THE ANXIETY TRILOGY

Gavin Roach

CURRENCY PRESS
The performing arts publisher

CURRENT THEATRE SERIES

First published in 2022
by Currency Press Pty Ltd,
PO Box 2287, Strawberry Hills, NSW, 2012, Australia
enquiries@currency.com.au
www.currency.com.au

in association with Gavin Roach

Copyright: *I Can't Say the F Word*, *The Measure of a Man,* and *Your Silence Will Not Protect You* © Gavin Roach, 2022.

COPYING FOR EDUCATIONAL PURPOSES
The Australian *Copyright Act 1968* [Act] allows a maximum of one chapter or 10% of this book, whichever is the greater, to be copied by any educational institution for its educational purposes provided that that educational institution [or the body that administers it] has given a remuneration notice to Copyright Agency [CA] under the Act.
For details of the CA licence for educational institutions contact CA, 11/66 Goulburn Street, Sydney, NSW, 2000; tel: within Australia 1800 066 844 toll free; outside Australia 61 2 9394 7600; fax: 61 2 9394 7601; email: info@copyright.com.au

COPYING FOR OTHER PURPOSES
Except as permitted under the Act, for example a fair dealing for the purposes of study, research, criticism or review, no part of this book may be reproduced, stored in a retrieval system, or transmitted in any form or by any means without prior written permission. All enquiries should be made to the publisher at the address above.

Any performance or public reading of *The Anxiety Trilogy* is forbidden unless a licence has been received from the author or the author's agent. The purchase of this book in no way gives the purchaser the right to perform the play in public, whether by means of a staged production or a reading. All applications for public performance should be addressed to the author c/-Currency Press

Typeset by Brighton Gray for Currency Press.
Cover image by Ali Choudry.
Cover design by Mathias Johansson for Currency Press.

Currency Press acknowledges the Traditional Owners of the Country on which we live and work. We pay our respects to all Aboriginal and Torres Strait Islander Elders, past and present.

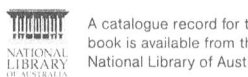

A catalogue record for this book is available from the National Library of Australia

Contents

THE ANXIETY TRILOGY

    I Can't Say the F Word   1

    The Measure of a Man   29

    Your Silence Will Not Protect You   55

Theatre Program at the end of the playtext

This play text went to press before the end of rehearsals and may differ from the plays as performed.

I Can't Say the F Word was first produced at The Owl and The Pussycat, Richmond, on 15 September, 2014, with the following creatives:

Writer and performer, Gavin Roach
Director, Lauren Hopley

***

The Measure of a Man was first produced at Gasworks Arts Park, Albert Park, on 1 February, 2016, with the following creatives:

Writer and performer, Gavin Roach
Director, Lauren Hopley

***

Your Silence Will Not Protect You was first produced at Meat Market Stables, North Melbourne, on 24 September, 2019, with the following creatives:

Writer and performer, Gavin Roach
Director, Lauren Hopley

I Can't Say the F Word

Lights up.

CELLARDOOR.
> Cellardoor.
> Cellardoor is,
> apparently,
> the most beautiful word in the English language.
> And I say apparently because I have no idea who actually conducts the surveys that determine facts like that.
> And who are the individuals that take part in them?
> I mean, I didn't.
> Did you?
> No really, did you?
> Anyone?
> No?
> Then how in the world was it voted the most beautiful word?
> What do you think?
> Does it steal your heart and whisk you away to romantic places afar?
> Or for you, does it simply mean 'open me up and you'll find booze'?
> I have to admit it does have a certain quality to it but my favourite word,
> the word that I enjoy saying the most, is justice.
> Justice.
> Say it with me,
> justice.
> Sounds great, right.
> Justice.
> It's like you have to use your whole mouth to say it.
> I like it because of the meaning behind it as well.
> Justice, striking truth into the hearts of men,
> and that's actually its official meaning.
> Other words I love to say are cut,
> chop,
> rush,
> elongate.

I like words that have an onomatopoeia quality to them.
And then there's doodle.
Doodle.
I love doodle.
Well, I mean, I love saying doodle.
It's hilarious.
Doodle.
Doodle.
Everyone now … doodle.
Great, right?
We all have our favourite words.
What are yours?

Point to audience members to shout out their favourite words.

I am fascinated by words.
Every day we are adding more and more words to the English vocabulary.
Changing existing words and creating new ones.
I set myself the task of finding out how many words there are in the English language.
I woke up with this curiosity.
I thought it would be an easy fact to find out.
A simple Google search and there the answer would be.
But the more I researched the harder it was to nail down an exact number.
Not even Wikipedia could help me and it got me through three degrees.
Yes that's right,
not only is the man standing before you ravishingly,
another good word,
good looking,
but he is also highly educated as well.
I have a BA in Acting,
Honours First Class in Directing,
and a Masters in Arts Management.
Put all of them together and my job prospects are still on par with that of a highly trained monkey.

During my quest to find the answer,
how many words are there,
I even went as far as to count all the words in the dictionary.
Actually that's a lie.
I did try,
I gave it a really good fist,
but I got about two pages into the As
and fell asleep.
It was so boring,
and would have taken me weeks to count them all.
What I have discovered however is that it is virtually impossible to pinpoint the exact number of words in the English language.
And there are two main reasons why.

Reason number one:
'Words we no longer use.'
There are countless words that,
over the centuries,
have fallen by the wayside.
Words that have gone out of style,
or words that just aren't relevant anymore.
As time went by and fashions changed,
we have lost so many truly awesome words.
Words like flibbertigibbet.
Flibbertigibbet is a word referring to a flighty or whimsical person, usually a young woman.
Flibbertigibbet,
how could anyone not say flibbertigibbet?
Try it; try saying flibbertigibbet and not giggle.
Come on try it with me,
flibbertigibbet.
See, brilliant.
And the fun doesn't stop there.
There are words like hugger-mugger.
Hugger-mugger means to act in a secretive manner.
Brabble, to argue loudly about something inconsequential.
Fuzzle, to make drunk or intoxicate.

Curmuring, a low rumbling sound produced by the bowels.
Gross.
Cockalorum, which means, a little man with a high opinion of himself.
And my new favourite word, groak.
Not only is groak an awesome word to say,
groak,
but its meaning elevates it above all other words.
Groak means to silently watch someone while they are eating,
hoping to be invited to join.
Think about it, how many times have you been sitting in a café and unknowingly been groaking someone.
I don't know why these words went out of style,
but for whatever reason these and so many other truly awesome words did.
Though I for one think that many of them are way overdue for a comeback.

Reason number two:
'New words.'
Just as quickly as some words vanish from use,
new ones pop up to take their place.
Every day new words are being made up and used.
Often they are abbreviations of other words or offshoots.
Words like snacky, meaning when one feels like a snack.
Blook, a blog writer who has written a book.
Then there's bromance,
overshare,
noughties,
selfie,
and everyone's favourite new word, twerk.
And then we have slumdog,
frape,
Zumba,
and smirt.

    Smirts to audience.

See?
See that?

I'm smirting at you right now.
Intrigued?
Yeah you are.
Smirting is when someone smirks and flirts,
at the same time.
Delicious.
A new word often simply starts off as slang.
And then before we know it,
that word becomes commonplace.
Or a new word can be created with a specific purpose in mind.
Incidentally that's actually how the longest word in the English language came about.
Honestly it's a fascinating story.
The longest word in the English language has thirty letters in it,
which are p-s-e-u-d-o-p-s-e-u-d-o-h-y-p-o-p-a-r-a-t-h-y-r-o-i-d-i-s-m
and want to hear me pronounce it?
Impress you with my powers of vocabulary?
Okay.
Pseudopseudohypoparathyroidism.
Pseudopseudohypoparathyroidism.
The history around this word is almost as remarkable as the word itself.
A group of people,
stoners no doubt,
got together and decided that since history favoured the brave they would make up the longest word in the English language,
and therefore find fame and glory.
See usually it's the other way around.
Usually a word is given to something to kind of sum up its meaning,
but with this word,
pseudopseudohypoparathyroidism,
although technically being the longest word in the English language,
when it was invented,
it meant nothing.
However it has since taken on a meaning.
The longest word in the English language now means silica poisoning.

Yes folks, the next time you ingest too much of that tasty silica,
no longer will you have to be dull when telling friends about your unfortunate situation.
Now you can hold your head up high,
and say you have pseudopseudohypoparathyroidism.

It does make you wonder
how many other words started out meaning one thing,
and then evolved into another.
I mean it still happens now.
Every day we strip a word of one meaning,
and then wrap something else around it,
and then it means something totally different.
Same word,
but now,
new.

So where has this slightly annoying attraction to words come from,
I hear you ask?
Well my fascination started because I can't say one word.
Just one.
Out of all the millions of words out there,
I can't say one simple word.
Well not simple.
The word I can't say isn't simple at all.

There are words that I don't like to say.
Words like 'poo', for example.
Poo I can't say without adding in a comedic intention.
'Poo.' See?
The word grosses me out and not because of what it means.
I can say crap or shit or feces or poop—poop I like to say,
but 'poo',
just can't do it.
A lot of people I know can't stand the word moist.
Moist.
A friend of mine flat-out refuses to say it and for another,
it's the moi … moi … moi … moi part of the word she can't handle.

Moist.
I personally don't mind it,
until it's put into context with cake.
I loathe it when people say,
'Oh this cake is moist!'
No it's not.
The cake is not damp or wet or dewy.
The cake is enchanting and scrumptious.
It certainly is not moist.
So in the spirit of creating a safe space,
I want you to shout out your most hated word.
Come on, now is not the time to be shy.
No judgment, just a collective togetherness.
A moment to bond as we reflect on the words that make us shudder.

   Audience shout out their most hated word.

There now,
don't we all feel better?
Don't we all feel all warm and fuzzy
now that we've shared with those around us?

Aaaaaand now getting back to word I can't say.
The word I can't say is the F word.
The F word.
Which isn't 'fuck' by the way.
I can say 'fuck'.
I love saying 'fuck'.
'Fuck, fuck, fuck.'
'Fuck' has to be my all time second favourite swear word.
My favourite swear word is the C word,
but you can't say that word in polite company.

   Mouths the C word.

So no, the F word isn't 'fuck'.
Then which F word could I mean?
Does anyone want to have a guess?
Anyone?
Just shout it out.

Don't be timid,
I won't be offended.
You won't be dragged up on stage.
Go ahead,
shout out what you think the F word is.

    Audience shouts out the F word.

Yes.
Perfect.
Correct.
That is indeed the F word that I can't say,
and now you are going to be part of the show.
Anytime I need the F word said,
I am going to point to you.
Okay?

Now, the F word.

    Points to audience member.

The F word has two traditional meanings associated to it.
The first is a ball or roll of seasoned chopped liver that is baked or fried.
I mean yum right.
Who doesn't love a—

    Points to audience member.

of baked liver.
And the second one,
the meaning that you're probably more familiar with, is
a bundle of sticks bound together as fuel.
Practical really,
if not a little outdated.
These are the two 'official' meanings of the F word,
but think about it.
It doesn't mean that anymore,
does it?
You wouldn't hear someone say—

    Points to audience member.

in regards to a bundle of sticks
nor would anyone use it when selecting their seasoned liver.
No, you're more likely to hear that word,
the F word—

Points to audience member.

said in reference to me.

When I was in Year Two,
I was teased relentlessly.
It had formed part of my school experience.
Every day I had to answer to the other students.
Justifying what I did,
who I was,
and why.
'Why do you play with the girls?'
'Because they're my friends.'
'Why don't you like to play football?'
'Because I like to dance.'
'Why are you a girl?'
'You're not a boy, you're a girl.'
'No, I'm a boy, I'm not a girl. I don't want to be a girl. I'm a boy … '
But they never listened.
I was a girl and that was that,
and no amount of arguing or pleading or begging was ever going to
    change their minds.
And that's how it was.
Every day.
It was pointless to fight back,
so I just became numb instead.
I accepted that that was just going to be part of my everyday,
and that the six hours I'd be at school were going to be filled with
    not-so-subtle attacks.
With each passing year another layer went up.
I built a wall around myself,
a wall that didn't keep them out,
but rather kept my agony in.
I once asked my mother,

'How do you kill yourself?'
I was eight.
I don't remember it but she does,
to this day,
she has never been able to forget it.
I never did though;
try to take my own life.
I didn't want them to win.
I didn't want them to break me,
to push me that far.
I never want to prove them right.

Whether we like to admit it or not,
children have a sixth sense when it comes to seeking out
or pointing out what's different.
I like to think that this comes from just a natural curiosity,
they question those around them who behave differently to their
    family or themselves,
but sometimes,
all too often,
many children are taught to see the differences in people,
and then to judge them,
for being not the norm …
well not their version of normal.
It pains me to say but my niece Ava,
she's ten,
made a comment at a family picnic recently that left me utterly
    speechless.
It was mother's day and she was running up to me and before I
    could hug her, she proudly said,
'Your brother calls you Captain Weirdo.'
I just looked to her,
shocked.
'And he also calls you … '
She never finished the sentence.
Her mother clamped her hand over her mouth and looked at me,
with a patronising smile.

I couldn't look at my brother for the rest of the afternoon.
If I was ballsier I would have confronted him,
demanded to know what he'd been saying about me,
but I already knew the answer to that.
Growing up my older brother never shied away from saying the F word—

Points to audience member.

He never said it directly to me; no he was much more subtle about it.
If we were playing a video game and I beat him,
he'd throw down the controller and say,
'Bloody—!'

Points to audience member.

He maintained it was directed at the computer character,
but it didn't take a genius to work out what he really meant.
I've never come out to him,
my brother,
and no he's not blind.
I tell people the reason why I haven't is that he never came out to me.
He never had to sit me down and say,
'I'm straight'
and then have to beg for acceptance.
That's what I tell people,
but the truth is,
I haven't told him because I'm terrified of him.
Terrified of how he will react.
My own brother.
He's my only sibling,
and he terrifies me.

By high school I could clearly see how different I was from other boys.
The dancing,
the acting,
the unspoken obsession with She-Ra, Princess of Power,
it all added up to what made me fabulous,

but it also me very different in the eyes of the other students.
It was like I got to the school with a huge target on my back.
Now the words were different.
Now I was different.
I feared the words they used because they did,
in a way,
on a very base level,
define me.
I was a very innocent boy growing up;
it took me a while to work out the world around me.
I never paid too much attention to my changing body,
or how others were changing around me.
I had always known who I was,
deep down,
what I felt,
it felt natural.
I was always going to be the way I am now,
standing here before you,
but back then,
with all those words used to define me,
I felt wrong.
I felt vulgar.
I felt scared.
I was always terrified going to school because I knew that they would know, that everyone would see just what I was,
and what I was, wasn't right.
I used to spend the long walk home asking myself,
'Are you? Are you what they say you are?'
'No!' I would scream on the inside.
'That is not what you are, not who you are.
You aren't what they say you are.
You aren't wrong.
You aren't vile.
You aren't fractured.
You're just a little bit different.
You just need to try harder.
Try to fit in.'

And try I did.
I got myself a girlfriend.
Enter Kylie Fletcher.
We would chat in English class from time to time,
and then one day I decided to take the plunge,
and ask her out.
So I wrote her a note.
A very simple note.
Direct and to the point.
'Would you like to go out with me? Yes/ No.'
She circled yes,
and that set the standard for our whole four-month relationship.
We would pass notes back and forth,
discussing very important topics,
like 'How was your day?'
And 'What class do you have next?'
At lunchtime we would nervously sit next to each other,
not saying a word.
We did hold hands once though,
but it was ...
she had really sweaty palms,
and that really grossed me out.
So in keeping with tradition,
I wrote her a note explaining why I didn't want to hold hands.
I didn't tell her the truth,
I'm not an idiot,
I can't really remember what I said but it worked.
From that day on I never had to hold her hand again.
We broke up at drama camp.
She dumped me.
Her exact words were,
'Ha ha, you're dumped. Suck shit.'
I was relieved.
After we broke up,
life just carried on like it always did,
and to this day Kylie Fletcher was my one and only girlfriend.
It didn't do much to quell the name-calling though,

having a girlfriend.
If anything it just gave the other students more to talk about.

When I was in Year Eight,
I decided to start to walk home from school.
It wasn't far,
thirty minutes,
twenty-five if I walked fast.
To pass the time,
I divided the walk up into five sections.
Each section had its own length,
and a clearly defined beginning and end point.
Section One was from school to the roundabout.
Section Two was from the roundabout to the bridge.
Section Three was the bridge.
Section Four was from the top of the bridge to the set of lights.
This section was always the hardest 'cause you could see the end point in the distance.
And the last section,
Section Five,
was from the traffic lights to home.
I used to talk to myself as a kid,
well actually I still do,
and I used to give myself a little pep talk,
to make it to the next section.
I'd distract myself,
focus on walking,
saying to myself out loud,
'Not far now, almost at Section Two.'
Or 'Section Three coming up,
you can slow down, Gavin,
just slow down.'
I could slow down in Section Three,
not because the bridge was overly steep,
which is was,
but because the bus had gone by,
and I could relax again.

The bus.
Bus Seventy-Seven.
Bus Seventy-Seven was this big bright yellow bus,
with rust spots,
and pumped out a really toxic-smelling odour.
Once the bell had rung,
it was an onslaught to get to the bus.
All the niceties of the day were gone.
We all shoved,
and pushed,
and left each other behind,
not caring if we would see each other again.
We only cared about getting on that damn bus.
And because I was small,
I could easily weave my way through the crowd,
and get to the front of the line.
But for all my ballsy skills,
there was a huge flaw in my plan.
See mine was the first stop,
and after I had proudly gotten myself onto Bus Seventy-Seven,
before the masses,
my first impulse was to race to the back of the bus.
I never sat in the back seat;
I wasn't that cool,
and the kids that did sit there would punch anyone who dared to take their place.
I usually sat a few seats back from the middle.
And it was my choice of seat on the bus that revealed the flaw in my plan.
Because mine was the first stop,
when it came time for me to get off the bus,
I had to run the gauntlet of other students.
Pushing and squeezing and shoving my way slowly,
very slowly,
down the length of the bus.
No-one wanted to move,
and no-one ever thought of getting off the bus,

letting me off,
and then getting back on.
No it was run the gauntlet or stay on the bus,
forever trapped in a sea of schoolbags and sweaty teenagers.
Once the bus doors whooshed closed and the vehicle lurched forward,
I was trapped.
Trapped with countless other students,
all hot and crammed together.
Students, who, once their eyes had settled to their new surroundings,
would hunt for their prey.
And that's usually when they found me.
Students,
from every year,
every age,
would point,
and jeer,
and shove,
and soon,
I no longer ran for the bus.
I let me feet drag and purposely took the long way round to the bus stop.
I wanted to remain unseen,
I stuck to the back of the crowd and waited,
until the very last person had gotten onto the bus before I boarded.
I feared running that gauntlet,
hearing the words spat at me,
sometimes even followed by a projectile of actual spit.
I endured that bus until one day,
during the holidays,
as the foreboding of returning to school sunk in,
my mother said,
'Why not walk to school, and just catch the bus only if you really have to.'
Suddenly it all seemed so simple.
Just walk.
I was saved.

I CAN'T SAY THE F WORD

Except between Sections One and Two.
You see,
between those Sections of the walk home,
Bus Seventy-Seven would drive by.
I worked out that if I made it past the roundabout and into Section Two,
I could handle it.
I could keep my head down,
and block out the oncoming bus.
Before the roundabout however,
the traffic used to bank back to the lights.
Bus Seventy-Seven would become stationary,
causing my walk past to become intolerable.
Hanging out of each of the windows was an indeterminable amount of students.
They would squeeze themselves out of the tiny bus windows,
screaming.
Those that couldn't fit would punch the windows instead.
Each one punching hard,
almost in unison.
Thump ... Thump ... Thump ...
That was the year I first heard it.
That was the year I first heard the F word—

Points to audience member.

It wasn't just the other students that I had to deal with.
More than a few teachers got in on the action too.
One particular was my PE teacher.
During one class,
in Year Ten,
we were divided up in to girls and boys,
like always,
and the girls went off to do skipping and the boys had to play football.
I was selected last for a team,
which really didn't bother me at all.
What bothered me more was that I wasn't allowed to go and skip.

I was good at skipping.
I enjoyed skipping.
I was better than half the girls skipping.
But being a boy,
I had to participate in the activities designated male.
The game started and I did what I thought was best for me team.
I stood as far away from the action as possible,
in the very far corner.
That way the best players would be in on the action and in turn,
prevent me from having any contact with the ball,
and therefore minimising my team's chances of losing.
Genius right?
Sadly it didn't play out according to plan.
There I was just casually counting the blades of grass,
and minding my own business,
when I heard this roar.
It was from the PE teacher.
He seemed to be screaming, 'Give the ball to Gavin.'
This concerned me,
his screaming,
mainly because I was afraid that somehow I had fallen asleep standing up,
and now I was having a nightmare.
But no,
I wasn't dreaming,
and I hadn't misheard him.
The ball was indeed heading my way,
and fast too.
I hoped that the other team members would see the look of horror on my face and interpret that as 'No … just … just no.'
But the teacher kept screaming for the ball to come to me.
It was all happening so fast.
My palms got sweaty and my mouth dried up.
I felt my face flush and my ears filled with the thump of my heartbeat.
Thirty metres,
twenty metres,
ten metres,

five metres.
In an instant my teammate with the ball was in front of me,
and the ball was thrown my way.
I watched,
almost in perfect slow motion,
as the ball sailed past me.
It bounced once,
twice,
and then settled into a roll as it continued along the field.
A few guys from my team pushed past me,
one knocking hard into my shoulder.
The teacher was furious.
He was red and running towards me.
'Why didn't you catch the ball, Gavin?'
'I'm sorry.'
That was all I could say without crying.
'Why didn't you try?'
'I'm sorry.'
'Do you want to go skip with the girls then, you fucking—

Points to audience member.

—do you?'
I was shaking by this point.
He was so close to my face,
and was trying so hard not to pass out.
He was a big man too.
Not fat but built.
Thick legs and broad shoulders,
olive skin and dark black hair,
cut short.
His dark brown eyes were furious.
My head was spinning and I was almost at the point of wetting myself.
There was however one thought running through my head.
A thought I chose not to say out loud.
I kept thinking, 'Is that an option?
Can I go and skip with the girls?

Because, I would like that.
I would like that very much.'
But I just stared at the ground and waited,
waited until he had his rant and then watched as he walked away,
shaking his head as he picked up the football.
I didn't tell my parents what happened,
what he said,
because nothing would have been done.
He may have been disciplined sure,
but I'd still have to be in his class.
See every time I sought out help,
I was told that teaching staff couldn't be everywhere at once,
or that the needs of one student couldn't distract from the needs of the student body as a whole.
And once,
once I was asked,
'Have you tried not standing out? Maybe if you weren't so obvious you wouldn't get picked on so much.'
Well I mean that does sound like an easy fix,
doesn't it?

Now every good fairytale needs a hero,
and I was lucky enough to have a few.
One was Nathan Clarke.
Nathan Clarke was probably the first guy in my life to just accept me
for who I was and not judge me or make assumptions.
And it was because of Nathan Clarke that I finally figured out my sexuality.
We first met when I was in Year Nine.
I had been wrestling with my feelings for most of that year,
and was totally terrified.
One day in cooking class,
my favourite subject,
Mrs Stoneham,
my cooking teacher,
announced that a new boy would be joining the class.

I had my head down,
diligently taking notes on the molecular structure of sugar.
Mrs Stoneham introduced him to the class and I raised my head,
so that I didn't seem rude.
I laid eyes on Nathan Clarke and my reaction was this,
'Oh!' 'Uh!' 'Ah! Fuck I'm gay.'
And that was when I knew.
Suddenly,
in an instant,
it all made sense.
The feelings,
the thoughts,
the wondering,
it was all standing there before me.
Standing there in all its very well-fitted school uniform glory.
Of course the only spare seat in the class was next to me,
so that's where Nathan Clarke sat.
He smiled at me,
and I tried hard not to vomit,
and from then on we became friends,
and stayed friends.
We still talk now,
though I have never told him about my high-school crush.
So if you do know him,
please do me favour,
for my sake,
and keep your mouth shut.

My other hero was my Year Ten cooking teacher,
Mrs Backers.
Mrs Backers was hilarious.
She had a casual approach to teaching,
casual but firm.
It was up to you to do the work and if you slipped up,
she let you have it.
By Year Ten I was acing my cooking subject.
I had come first in the class every year,

and nothing and nobody was going to stop my dream run.
Tara Birril tried to beat me one year and she,
well she ended up with a salty cake.
It's not my fault that she can't tell the difference between her white granules.
In Year Ten,
Mrs Backers and I bonded because I used to sneak off from my PE class.
My cooking class was after PE so I figured I could get a head start on the day's activities.
I still had my horrible PE teacher—

Points to audience member.

so on days when we were forced to participate in the outdoor activities,
I used to take up my place on the side of the field.
and when no-one was looking,
I'd casually just wander off,
head to the cooking classroom,
and make a cake.
The first time I did it,
Mrs Backers gave me an odd look as I was sifting my flour and asked, 'Shouldn't you be at PE?'
'Yeah,' I said,
staring at her,
hoping she wouldn't force me to go back to class.
She just shot me a sly smile,
and told me to clean up after myself when I was done.
And that's how it stayed for the whole rest of the year.
My PE teacher caught me once though.
I was in the middle of creaming my butter and sugar when suddenly,
the classroom door flew open and he stormed in,
red faced and puffing.
He glared at me and said, 'Get back to the field you little—'

Points to audience member.

I was just about to concede defeat when Mrs Backers walked out from the storeroom.

She locked eyes with him and very calmly said,
'Oh I don't think he's going anywhere.'
My PE teacher went a deep scarlet shade,
but Mrs Backers held her ground.
'We're done here,' she said, 'get back to your students.'
He went wide-eyed and then turned on his heel and left,
slamming the door behind him.
Mrs Backers let out a tiny little giggle,
shook her head,
looked at me and said,
'Careful you don't overmix your batter, Gavin.'
'Yes miss,' I said, eyes welled up with tears.
Mrs Backers was my cooking teacher for the next three years.
She pushed me to be a better cook and gave me something to cling
    to,
hope.
She even went as far as to ban the F word from her classroom.

Things are very different now.
It's been over ten years since I graduated high school,
and many have embraced it,
the F word.
Liberally saying it without fear.
It really is just a word to them—

Points to audience member.

As common as words like 'the', 'had' or 'was'.
A lot of people say that they are reclaiming it.
Giving it a more positive spin.
Because,
after all,
it is just a word and we can,
ultimately,
choose its meaning or intent.
That's something I don't understand.
It might be me and my feelings toward the word,
but I can't understand how you can reclaim something that didn't
    have that meaning to begin with.

This word was forced upon us,
or rather the new meaning was.
How can anything positive come from that?
And in what positive way can you say that word?
There really is no nice way to use it.
It's the vulgarity of the word,
the F word—

> *Points to audience member.*

that makes it stick in my throat.
It feels heavy in my mouth.
It's sound,
the way the F word sounds, is harsh,
violent,
there's a savagery to it.
It's like it has to be spat out,
dripping with venom.
Spat out from behind cruel and gnashing teeth.

I often wonder how a word that used to mean a simple bunch of sticks
took on the meaning it has today.
How did it change?
And why?
What is it about a bunch of sticks,
or a stack of seasoned liver that made someone,
somewhere, think
'Hey that is the perfect word to use to insult so-and-so down the road.'
And then somewhere along the way,
at some tiny moment in history,
the F word—

> *Points to audience member.*

stopped meaning a bunch of sticks altogether and became a word of hate.
And no-one stopped it.
Or if they did,

it fell on deaf ears.
I'm sure that many tried,
tried to fight back and say,
'No that's not right. You can't call me that.'
But the wheels of intolerance kept turning,
and the word that once meant a humble bunch of sticks,
was gifted with a brand-new offensive meaning—

   Points to audience member.

Someone once asked me,
why was I so angry when it came to the F word?
I didn't even realise that I was coming off angry.
I didn't,
and still don't,
like the word—

   Points to audience member.

but angry,
that was news to me.
But they were right.
I am angry.
I'm angry because I was never allowed to fight back.
I just had to take it,
and that's where this anger towards the F word comes from.
So many times I kept hearing,
'Just walk away. Be the bigger man and walk away.'
Or the delightfully helpful,
'Just ignore them. Don't listen to them when they say hurtful things.'
Don't listen?
Just don't listen?
Because it's easy to do that.
It's easy to block out the screaming and the insults.
Easy to listen and just walk away,
forgetting everything that has just been said to you.
And its soooo easy to not scream 'Why?' in the faces of the people
   doing it.
Why?
Why did they, or anyone for that matter,

feel that they could get away with it?
I mean,
I know why,
but I wanted them to have to justify it.
I wanted more than anything a chance for them to be accountable for their actions.
And to have to say why and really let that sink in.
I hate that they got to me,
that I am left with these wounds that aren't going to heal.
Left with memories and words,
well one word—

Points to audience member.

that still haunts me.
Still affects me,
even after all these years.

I can't say the F word,
but the truth is I could.
I could form the word,
and let it slip from my mouth.
I could hurl it out,
and not care who heard.
But I won't.
There's a very big difference between I can't,
and I won't.
I won't say it.
I won't say the F word.

Snap to black.

THE END

The Measure of a Man

Lights up.

The first time I measured my penis I was thirteen years old.
I did it one afternoon after overhearing how some girls at school had dared a friend of theirs to measure his.
But he had to measure it on the flop.
How awesome is that phrase,
'on the flop'.
So,
that afternoon I went to my room,
shut the door,
took out my ruler,
and for the very first time,
I measured myself.
And at thirteen years of age my penis measured in at two-point-three centimetres or one-point-two inches.
I don't know why most guys will give you their measurements in inches,
being that bigger is ultimately better,
but when it comes to penis size,
most guys prefer the imperial unit of measurement.
So that was my penis at thirteen years of age,
and though the years have gone by,
not much has changed.
Right now,
today,
my penis measures in at three-point-two centimetres or two-point-one inches.
On the flop.
Erect however,
my penis measures in at seventeen-point-one centimetres or six-point-seven inches,
which is above average.
The average global penis size is five-point-five inches,
making my erect six-point-seven-inch penis,
above average.

Making me,
above average.

When I was growing up,
I paid very little attention to my penis.
To me its only real purpose was that I peed out of it.
That's about as much thought as I cared to give it,
well apart from cleaning it every morning and evening.
I'm uncircumcised you see.
Side note—you wouldn't believe how many guys are fascinated by foreskin.
And some guys have even fetishised it.
It's like,
for some guys,
knowing that I have a foreskin seals the deal.
There was one guy who was totally enthralled by mine.
He would sit there,
playing with it,
just staring at it,
massaging it.
At first it was kind of hot but, actually no,
it was always just rather awkward.
I was always laying there wondering if I should look up and suggest that they should get a room.
And if I wasn't attached to it,
I think he would have done just that.

I did start paying attention to it,
my penis,
when I was seventeen years old.
But not in the way that you might think.
It had begun to change,
well actually my testicles had begun to change,
not so much my penis.
I had developed a growth.
A growth that had started growing over the years and now,
at seventeen,

it had started to look ugly,
jagged.
It had started to look like this spongy brain-like mass wrapped in scrotum skin hanging between my legs.
That was the first time I looked at myself,
and thought,
'What is someone else going to think of this?
What will they think of me?'
It wasn't anything serious,
but it would need to be removed.
It was just a build-up of fluid,
a build-up that had started when I was eight years old.
A build-up that was caused by an ill-timed basketball to the testicles.
I was in primary school and Debbie Harris hurled a basketball my way,
and thwack,
bang,
she got me right in the goddamn balls.
It wasn't an instant hurt,
no,
no,
no,
it was more like a dull thud.

Days later the pain was still there,
so off to the doctor we went,
and next thing I knew my pants were down around my ankles,
and a nurse was dumping half a bottle of what I now know is K-Y Jelly on my balls.
My GP had recommended an ultrasound,
just to be sure,
and thankfully the nurse gave me the all-clear,
never knowing that nine years later I'd need full-blown surgery.
No,
she just smiled at me,
told me it was done,
and then tossed me one tiny piece of tissue,

and told me to clean myself up.
That tiny piece of tissue didn't go very far,
so I spent the entire car ride home with moist underwear,
reeking of K-Y Jelly—
a sensation that I would become very accustomed to later in life.
Flashforward nine years and there I am,
lying on a hospital bed,
as a nurse prepares to shave my wispy pubic hair,
while a room full of doctors decide how best to remove the lumps.
It was a simple operation really,
just a cut in the groin,
then they pull out the testicle,
cut out the lumps,
stitch the wounds,
stuff the testicle back in,
and then stitch up the groin.
Easy.
I even have a scar.
I was feeling fine in a few days and best of all,
best of all,
when I looked down,
it actually looked like something that I'd want someone else to see.
Something I'd be happy to show someone else.
But not touch.
No.
At seventeen years old I didn't want anyone,
guy or girl,
to touch me.

***

The first time I touched another man's penis I was eighteen years old.
I was at university and every week a group of us would drag our blankets into the common room and watch *Buffy*.
Me and another guy in the group used to lie next to each other,
and then one night,
very casually,

our hands started to wander.
It was very slow at first.
A brush of bare skin.
The slow unzip of the fly.
The nervous creeping of fingertips under the waistband of underwear.
He was a lot more experienced than I was,
but for me,
contained in that moment,
was a world of firsts.
He shifted his body so I could slip my hand further in,
and then,
I held it.
His penis felt so different from my own.
Fat and veiny.
Uncircumcised but wet.
Wet and sticky.
And I just held it.
And held it.
And held it.
Honestly I didn't know what else to do.
I just held it till *Buffy* was finished and then we rapidly did up our pants and that was that.

***

A year later would be the first time I took a guy home.
We met at a house party and got along famously.
So we get back to mine and I pointed to my bedroom,
before going to the bathroom to pee,
and do my 'there is a man in my house' dance.
A dance that looks like this.
A dance that I still do,
to this very day,
whenever I have a man inside my house.
I walk back into my room,
get into bed,
and realise,
he's pantsless.

Unexpected.
We made out and fumbled around for an exhausting twenty minutes,
until he straddled me and said,
'I think we should cum.'
I gave him an odd look,
and in all seriousness I asked,
'What's that?'
Honestly,
I didn't know what he was talking about.
And he just laughed at me,
and laughed
and laughed some more,
and then stared at me,
got off me,
and curled up over the other side of the bed.

***

Six months later I lost my boy virginity.
Not to that guy,
no,
no,
no to my boyfriend at the time.
A guy much younger than me but again,
much more experienced.
I was living on my own at that point,
because my housemate had gone crazy and moved back in with her parents, and it was the first time that his parents had let him stay over.
We were each other's firsts so it was going to mean something.
It was going to be special.
We were both making such a big deal about who was going to do what till finally,
I decided to just settle the issue,
and sit on it.
So, half a tube of K-Y Jelly and a full bottle of Merlot later,
I found myself manoeuvering his penis slowly,
very slowly,

so he could enter me.
And I was doing everything right.
Breathing,
relaxing,
unclenching,
anticipating the oncoming pain,
I had heard so much about the pain.
But see the thing with anal sex is,
once you get over the pop,
the pop is when your body opens up and you are able to take in the head of the penis,
once you get over that,
the rest is just rather easy.
Well, it is for me anyway.
After the pop,
I slowly eased myself down the length of his penis.
Slowly gliding down,
preparing myself for the pleasure.
But after a moment,
my boyfriend gave me the oddest look.
'I'm all in' he said.
'Yeah, I know' I said back.
'No, I'm all in' he said again,
this time with a little bit more conviction.
And he was,
he was completely inside me.
And I felt nothing,
no pain,
no pleasure.
It was like I wasn't being let in on the joke.
Surely I was meant to feel something, anything.
Something more than 'Oh so that's what a dick in your arse feels like.'
I didn't let on; of course,
I played the happy and dutiful boyfriend,
and just faked it.
I've had to fake it a lot over the years.

I pulled a Meryl.
Pulling a Meryl is when you stare at the wall,
focus,
steady yourself,
and then you throw yourself back,
and go for the Oscar.
You give the best performance of your life,
and make sure that they never know that deep down,
deep down you are just counting down the minutes,
waiting for it all to be over.
After my boyfriend was done,
I just got off and lay there.
He wanted to be held and was beaming with pride.
And I just stared at the ceiling,
wondering if it was ever going to get any better.
It didn't.
Not with that guy anyway.
I was with that guy for nine months and in that entire time I came a total of three times.
I was horribly naïve and just so,
grateful,
to have a boyfriend,
to have someone interested in me.
To have someone to touch me.

***

Upside though,
that was year that I started masturbating for the first time.
Seriously,
I was twenty before ever I touched myself.
Honestly,
up until then,
I never really felt the urge.
I wasn't like other boys I knew,
talking about it or touching it.
I got erections sure,
but I never partnered that with being turned on.

Maybe it was because I was scared or,
maybe I just didn't want to admit my oncoming sexuality.
My body took care of itself however.
Some mornings I'd wake up feeling utterly relaxed and horribly sticky,
and that was enough for me.
All of those urges,
that surging teenage sexual desire seemed to just pass me by,
but when it hit,
when I was twenty,
god it was like I was thirteen again.
I was doing it maybe three, four times a day,
And sometimes,
sometimes I'd even sneak off on my lunch break at uni to get it done.
But even with all the pulsing urges deep down,
deep down I wanted nothing more than to just kiss a guy.
Really kiss him.
Soft slow kisses,
the kind that you never want to end.
The kind of kisses where they reach up and cup your face.
Kisses like that …

***

When boyfriend and I broke up I started engaging in casual sex.
That boozy,
hedonistic phase when you make terrible choices,
but you're just so very thankful that anyone would even agree to follow you home.
It was during this time that things started to change.
A realisation,
an understanding that the way I looked and thought about my body was different to how others saw it.
And they weren't exactly shy about telling me either.

'I thought you'd be bigger.'
'I guess it's cold in here.'
'I'm just not turned on enough to follow through now.'

Most guys had the decency to just keep their mouths shut,
but one night,
one boozy drunken night,
I decided to cross the hallway and go into my housemate's room.
We'd been flirty all night so I just thought,
'Well why the fuck not.'
We spooned,
and then we made out,
and I touched him,
and he touched me,
and no … wait … stop …
then I came in my underwear.
And he laughed.
A great big hooting laugh-out-loud laugh.
I laughed too.
'Cause it was funny … it's funny.

A few weeks later were at the pub with friends.
My roommate comes back from the bar with drinks.
He puts the drinks down,
and out of nowhere said,
'You know what's funny about premature ejaculation?'
Turning to face me, eyes boring in.
'Nothing,' he said.
We all had a real good laugh that night.

***

London.
A nightclub.
Far away from … anything.
From everything I knew.
A sticky dance floor.
The throb of the beat.
And I'm dancing with a man.
And he is beautiful.
My height.
Brown hair.

THE MEASURE OF A MAN

Cheeky smile,
and a chest for days.
And he can move.
We dance and twirl together,
as the lights dart and spin around us,
and I am right where I want to be.
He goes to get us drinks and I follow,
I'm trusting but I'm smart.
We lean on the bar,
and talk,
and kiss,
and hold hands,
and laugh.
And I'm right where I want to be.
He suggests we go upstairs.
It's darker.
There's more privacy.
Nothing sleazy just somewhere to sit down.
So,
I follow him up the stairs,
and we sit.
And we kiss,
and we move closer,
and I slip my hand under his shirt,
and oh god, his chest.
And he grabs at my pants,
and struggles to undo my fly.
I let out a giggle,
and he smiles as he kisses me.
He slips his hand into my pants,
and then he stops.
He stops kissing me.
He's frozen in the moment.
He moves his body away from mine,
removing his hand last.
'I'm empty,' he says,
gesturing with a still half-full glass.

He downs the rest of his drink,
gets up,
and goes back downstairs,
and I wait.
I wait and I watch.
I watch him dance with another man.
Leave with another man.
I get up and I head downstairs,
I rejoin the dance floor,
And let the thump of the music sweep me up,
and I am back,
and I am right where I want to be.

***

It's been years since I've had a decent erection,
one that wasn't assisted by the miracles of science.
One that I could be proud of.
I mean I get them,
they do happen,
just not the way I'd like,
the way I'd want.
I start out strong enough,
firm and throbbing,
feeling the pulse of the blood shoot through my veins.
It's kind of hot to see the veins darken with your overly excited blood.
I imagine …
I imagine the red blood cells all strutting down the vein,
strutting like a bunch of drag queens heading to the club.
But then the throbbing wanes and I'm left with a flaccid mound of skin and shame.

***

'*Are you even going to get hard?*'

'*Touch me. It will work if you just touch me.*'

***

It was my ex,
the second one—I've only ever had two—
that said—'If we can't have sex then what is the point of being together?' We'd been fighting a lot, and I didn't know where all this was coming from.
But finally he opened up.
He rang.
He did it over the phone.
The conversation was calm at first.
Pleasant even,
but then,
then out of nowhere he just got so angry.
He started saying things like,
'Why are you doing this to me?
You don't know how important it is to me!
I need you to try!
Why aren't you trying?'
I had no idea what he was talking about but … .
But I did,
and it was my fault.
He caught me off guard,
and I said that the reason I couldn't get …
that I wasn't getting …
that I was letting my problem get in the way was …
I said that it was him …
and he got so angry.
He kept on yelling down the phone and I just wanted to scream at him,
scream at him to listen,
listen to what I wasn't saying.
I'd never said it before,
I'd never dared to,
but now I needed to.
I needed him to listen,
I needed him to understand,
I needed him to care.
I needed him.

***

But he was right.
And it was my fault.
I just stayed silent and let him say what needed to be said.
He ended the call with an ultimatum,
that if I couldn't get hard then,
the relationship,
me,
well it just wasn't worth the effort.
We broke up,
he ended it.
He ended it and I just …

I didn't want to think about it.
I was in control,
in control of my body.
I just had to keep on going.
Just had to keep on pushing through.
I just gotta get back on the horse and keep on riding.
Men would come over and I would be ready.
I had a system.
I would point them to my room,
and then say something like, 'Ooof, I need to pee.'
This bought me time.
I would go to the bathroom,
stand in the centre of the room,
count to ten,
do the dance,
and then if upon my return,
if they,
the men,
were in their underwear or less,
then there really wasn't much to talk about,
but if they were still fully clothed,
then I had to put in a little more effort.
We'd talk,
and flirt,

then—boom,
pants off fun times.

I was always so in control.

***

*Four a.m.
A man came over.
I invited him over.
He followed me up the stairs.
We kissed.
He bit my lip.
Threw me onto the bed.
Cracked one of the slats.
Asked if I had neckties.
Neckties to tie me down.
I tried to get up.
He hit my sternum.
I was winded.
I tried to get up.
He was overpowering.
'You got thirty seconds to get out mate or I'm coming in.'
She didn't wait though.
The door burst open and there she was,
my housemate,
fuming and ready for a fight.
He left and I just lay there,
naked,
exposed.
No man has ever touched me like that again.*

***

'Don't you like me?'

I've heard that a lot from guys over the years.
When my ... kicks in or doesn't,
they think it's them,
that it has something to do with them.

They crave a kind word,
a soft touch,
a warm embrace.
Reassurance.
Bless.

***

I have a system though.
A way to scoot round the awkwardness and keep the passion going.
I shift my body beside them,
turning my pelvis into the mattress,
rest of my body turned to face them.
I let my hand glide over them,
feeling them submit to the pleasure,
to the attention.
Some move against me,
but I am well versed in the art of the sleight of hand.
I swiftly move from their mouth to their body and back.
I am calm and in control,
maneuvering from their mouth to their body and back,
all the while my mind is going a mile a minute.
My head is always fuzzy when it comes to sex.
'What is he thinking?'
'Is my body okay?'
'Is he comfortable?'
'Am I doing it the way he likes?'
More and more I retreat to my head.
Anxiety building,
deafening my ears,
my inner monologue pulses,
a rolling cascade of static.
Relax, I keep thinking, relax,
but I …

I don't like where the placement of the pillow is.
Or, please god don't let him lick my ear.

And don't let him touch me.
Oh, why do guys think that biting down on your nipple is hot?
It's not hot.
Then there's the breath.
Is that taste him or me?
Him?
Me?
Him or me or him or me or him or ...
Urgh it's me.
Great no really,
dig your elbow into my hip,
'cause that's comfortable.
And now the sheet has fallen on an odd angle and my foot's stuck.
And don't let him touch me.
And is this it, is this all we are going to do, foreplay?
Are we going to have sex though?
What if he wants to?
Will he expect me to bottom,
'cause that, I just, I don't know how prepared I am ...
and I don't want to keep on faking it,
and oh god, if he wants me to top,
and what if I don't meet his ...
and what if he sees that I'm not what ...
Wait, stop, where's his hand going.
No, he can't.
He can't slide it there.
No.
Turn your body.
Shift it away.
Don't let him touch me.
Don't let him touch me.
Don't let him touch me.
Don't let him touch me.
Don't let him touch me.
Don't let him touch me.

Don't let him touch me.
Don't let him touch me ...

But I make sure they have a really good time.

***

The first doctor I went to said that he couldn't help because he didn't like to deal with those kinds of issues.
I had decided to open up,
to talk to someone about it.
It was eating away at me.
I had gone in there for my three-monthly blood tests,
and when I finally choked the words up,
he actually looked embarrassed for me.
Disgusted.
Angry that I would ask him about an issue like that.
After the nurse took my blood,
I found myself standing in a public bathroom stall,
trying not to scream,
eyes streaming with frustrated tears.
In that moment I'd never felt so tense.
So alone.
But the second doctor, he listened.

***

The first time I took Viagra,
it was,
disappointing.
As soon as I bought the packet,
I wanted to see if it would work.
If I would work.
I wasn't seeing anyone at the time and wasn't even trying to ...
So, I got on the apps and I was not subtle.
I was forward and crass and filthy and ...
and it worked.
A guy took the bait and I broke out in a nervous sweat.
I pushed my dirty clothes under the bed,
took the pill,

peed,
made the bed,
peed again,
and then he arrived.
We chatted for a bit,
and made out,
and moved to the bed,
and it was …
And it was just like all the other times.
He wanted it to be about him, about his needs.
He touched me, sure, but it was only enough to be polite.
I spent the whole time at half-mast,
holding back my mix of laughter and tears.
He left before I was done and I saw little reason to finish the job.

***

You honestly expect to get instantly hard.
This firm and throbbing cock protruding from your groin.
And you do, get hard, but it still takes its time.
You still have to be turned on.
And all the blood rushes to your head and you get kind of woozy,
like you're a little bit drunk.
And my face always goes red too.
And thirsty, god do you get thirsty.

***

I was drying my clothes in the laundromat when it hit me,
the urge.
So I grabbed my still damp clothes from the dryer,
ran home,
threw the clothes on the floor,
raced to the bathroom,
opened the drawer,
rustled around for the hiding spot,
popped one simple pill out of its plastic casing.
Stared at it.
Swallowed it,

gulped down some water.
And then waited.
Waited for the effect.
And when it hit,
I hurled myself on my bed,
Tore off my underwear,
and I gripped my penis.
And it was hard and firm and I swear it felt hot.
It was radiating heat.
I took my time and felt the skin glide under my hand.
The sensation rippled through my body and I shuddered.
I kept thinking,
'Is this how it feels for everyone else, every other guy?
Is this what it must feel like to be, normal?'

***

I don't know how other guys do it,
how they can be so confident.
When I am around other men I think,
'You bastard.
You fucking lucky bastard.'
'Cause you'll never know.
You'll never have to think about your body failing you time and time
 again. They'll never know the humiliation or the disappointment,
the anger or the envy.
It's the envy that …
I feel this rage when I am around other men.
When I hear them talk about their conquests,
their confidence,
their calm assured demeanor.
I just want to rip and crawl into them,
scratching at their skin and plunging into them to find it.
Find out what makes them more of a man than me.
I want so much to be a part of that world.
To feel bold and strong and powerful where it counts.
See I can talk it up,
sex,

my way with sex.
I am good at that.
Flirting about what I would do and how and all the many many ways I would get a guy off.
When asked what I'm into,
I will happily offer up a detailed list of all the various kinks and quirks that tickle my fancy.
But it's just talk, nothing but talk and wishful thinking.
I could never live up to their expectations.

***

I try not to think about it.
Over the years I have painted myself as a prude,
rather than deal with anyone on even the most remotely sexual level.
If it comes up in conversation,
I just brush it off,
feigning disinterest,
and let the conversation carry on without me.
I just don't want to talk about it.
The times I have brought it up I tend to get—
'Just have sex, it's easy.'
'Just keep on doing it till you find your rhythm.'
'Just do it. It's really not meant to be that hard.'
Actually it is.
It is meant to be hard.
It's meant to work.
I can't be the only one that feels this;
I can't keep living this shame alone.
It's the fear that eats away at you.
Fear that someone will find out and then ... everyone will.
And then the fear turns into shame,
and then you are lost to it.
You think that maybe you should give into all the hurt and the shame,
the anger and the envy.
And then you think that maybe you should just ...

I don't know how to make it go away.

***

I don't feel like I have a lot to offer someone,
a guy,
a guy that might be interested in me.
The more and more I engage with men,
the more it seems that sex is,
well it's just so important,
isn't it.
A deal-breaker,
something to be decided on from the onset.
Work out the sexual compatibility before actually getting to the sex,
'cause otherwise,
well 'cause otherwise,
what's the point right?
I'd like to be better at it.
To connect that way but it feels like,
well it's like when you go for a job and they say that you don't have the experience,
but are you able to gain the experience if you don't have the opportunity to do the job.
If I can't have sex,
if I can't connect in that way,
then what do I have to offer someone?
What worth do I have?

***

There was a guy.
Once.
And it was fun and relaxed and he seemed to understand.
I was … nervous and anxious and my body failed me time and time again, but … he just …
And every time I tried to go through my usual systems, he just …

We had spent the night watching movies and then,
in the wee small hours of the morning we crawled into bed,
and he held me,
and we kissed.

And soon the sheets were thrown to the side and I was slowly pushing back,
sliding my way into position.
Body facing away but still in control,
in control of him and what we were going to do ...
but ... he pushed back.
Gently.
So gently and soft and he kissed me so deeply.
He slid his body closer to mine and slipped his arm under my back, drawing me closer.
With the other hand he glided himself over my body.
So slowly that I just melted into the bed.
I was shaking and there was a part of me that was still so scared but it was silenced,
he silenced every thought I had and held me in that moment.
The kisses grew deeper and I was pulled closer still.
I could feel him firmly shift himself to be by my side and we molded and manoeuvered ourselves around one another.
With one hand under my head and the other gliding over me,
he subdued every fear,
every thought.
And then he touched me;
he held me and was put off or turned off.
He just kissed me harder,
softer and took control.
The feeling rippled over me.
It was ... suddenly about me ...
he wanted to touch me ...
to hold me ...
to kiss me ...
he wanted the moment to just totally be about me ...
and about us ...
together.
And soon it all built up ...
and when I did,
I tried to do what I always used to do ...
making those exaggerated noises and groans ...

biting my lip or gnashing my teeth ...
the sex face I have long practised. But he stopped me.
'Shhhh,' he said, kissing me into a soft and comforting silence.
We held that moment,
he made me hold that moment.
He cupped my face and we kissed and he slowly nuzzled into my neck and we fell asleep,
sticky and sweaty and...

And then, in the morning, he walked away.
He left.
He didn't want to be together anymore.
He didn't want to be with me.

When I look in the mirror,
I see a broken man looking back.
Shattered into a thousand pieces,
and I don't know how to put myself back together.

But I'm above average,
so that's got to count for something, right?

    Snap to black.

THE END

Your Silence Will Not Protect You

The first,
and only time,
I ever fisted someone,
I had a panic attack.
When I woke up that morning I never intended to fist anyone,
I don't think anyone does.
Actually,
no,
I dare say that there are probably a large number of people who would start their day with the intention to fist someone and more power to them.
No shame here.
But on this particular day,
fisting someone to my forearm certainly wasn't on my agenda.

The day started out like any other,
though it was my day off,
so I had longer than usual to lounge in bed.
But rapidly my need to pee forced me out of my comfortable cocoon and into the world.
I showered,
I peed … at the same time …
Uber Eats'ed a coffee,
made a little breakfast,
and then nestled into the couch.
Utter bliss.
But then my phone beeped.
Loudly.
Cutting through my morning bliss.

The message was from a friend.
Well, more an acquaintance.
A person I happen to know.
We'd made out a few times before but that didn't exactly make us anything more than what we were.
I opened the message and it said just one sentence …

'I've just been fired ... '
Well that's a bit shit then isn't it?

We bounced messages back and forth for a bit,
me making sure he was okay without prying too much and him ...
I think he was in shock.
I asked if he needed anything and he asked if I was up for company
    and if I didn't mind him coming round.
Frustrating as it was,
I forfeited my much-coveted day off to help the needy.
I'm basically a saint.

I sent my address,
and he said he'd be twenty minutes,
and twenty-five minutes later,
he arrived.
I hate when people are late.
We sat on the couch and talked and I made coffee and I have never
    seen someone look so panicked.
Both of us were avoiding the subject,
until a silence descended upon us both,
which was my cue to say—
'So, what happened?'

And how I was hoping that it would be something dramatic.
Something saucy.
Something delicious but,
instead,
it was so mundane.
Turned up late,
too many times.
Didn't get the work done,
too many times.
Was rude to customers,
too many times.
I mean,
what did he expect?
I'd fire him too.

But,
I nodded,
and sighed,
and said I see,
and nodded some more.
To be honest I was beginning to regret responding to his first message.
I get that it's shit but this was not how I wanted to be spending my day off.

I didn't think he was ever going to stop talking until finally,
he just looked at me,
stared at me for an increasingly unsettling amount of time,
and then said, 'I have to go to the bathroom,'
and he got up and left and I welcomed the silence.
I heard the flush,
and then the door opened,
and I didn't think much of it when he appeared in the lounge room again …
expect that now he wasn't wearing any pants.

'Where did your pants go?' I gasped.
He responded with a smirk and sat back down next to me,
closer than before.
Much closer than before.
He was wearing a jockstrap though.
Pink,
with yellow trim.
Did he wear that to work?
But that's really none of my business.
He started to angle himself towards me,
presenting his butt in a very birdlike display,
trying to attract my attention.
And it worked.
It wasn't long till we were making out and I was whispering,
'Let's move this to my bedroom.'
That wasn't me trying to be all sexy,
but rather simply following the rules.

My housemates and I had agreed that there is to be be no sexy times anywhere in the house apart from your own bedroom or the shower,
and only if the water is running,
and because I am a stickler for the rules,
I was insistent that we move to my bedroom.

Once there,
the kissing became more intense.
My clothes came off,
as did his.
All but the jockstrap.
Hands were going everywhere,
gliding and playfully grabbing.
It wasn't the worst but honestly I was still a little put out that this was interrupting my day off.
He asked if I had any lube and I got out my dainty small bottle and he giggled at me as I passed it to him.
'What?' I asked, impishly.
'Nothing, I'm just used to using a two-litre pump bottle for my lube.'
Right.
Okay.
Yes.
Um.
Right.
Right.
Right.
Right.

He applied the desired amount of lube to the area and I slipped in a digit.
'Another' he gasped.
So I did.
'More' he said.
So I popped in one more.
'You can fit more in,' he moaned,
very confidently.

He can't mean that we are to.
Surely we aren't.
It's just that I have never.
'All in' he said,
'All the way.'
So I dabbed a little more lube on my hand and started to slide in.
I didn't know what he expected me to do because it felt like there was no way in hell that my hand was going to go any further.
'Just relax,' he said,
calmly,
soothingly.
Relax?
You want me to relax?
How the hell am I to relax …
but he was right.
My hand was way too tense,
ridged.
Once I breathed into it,
loosened my grip,
softened the stiffness,
my hand was able to just kind of—

    Make a wet whooshing sound.

right on in.

And then,
I was inside him.
His eyes rolled back into his head and his body rippled with joy.
His face expanded into an ecstatic smile and I just kept on thinking,
'Well this is certainly not where I expected my day to end up.'

The hairs on the back of my neck started to prick up,
my mouth was dry,
I was sweating …
a lot.
I didn't quite know what was happening but then I realised …
I was having a panic attack.

***

I'm standing in a supermarket,
in the milk aisle.
See when I tell this story to people,
for some reason I say that I am in the milk aisle,
but I'm not.
I'm in the cereal aisle.
I'm looking at box after box and thinking about which I should get.
Should I go for a healthy one or treat myself.
Suddenly and without warning,
the world shifts,
on its axis,
to the left.
It tips and I turn cold.
The hairs along my arms prickle and I am breathing shallow.
I grip the handle of my trolley and my knuckles turn white.
I am rapidly breathing in,
but not out.
Sharp inhales,
one after the other,
causing my stomach to pucker with each breath.
I'm sweaty and cold and an unnerving vibration is increasingly shifting my focus inward.
I have to leave but I don't know what to do.
I don't know what is happening.
I feel like I should be crying,
but it is like someone has reached up from the ground,
twisted their hand around my insides,
and dragged them out.
I'm hollow.
I'm standing in a supermarket,
in the cereal aisle,
and I am having my first remembered panic attack.

I am twelve years old and I am sitting with my brother and sister-in-law at a family gathering.
It's someone's birthday or an anniversary,

I'm not sure,
but it's an event that warrants the whole family to attend.
We don't have much to do with this side of the family but respect is
    respect and family is family.
My brother is talking to me but I'm only half-listening,
because I am being watched.
Pointed at.
Pointed out.
Over to my left,
in my peripherals,
are cousins,
I think,
and they are pointing and laughing.
Pointing and laughing at me.
I have absolutely no idea what I have done or what they could be
    laughing at,
but they are,
and they just keep on going.
More join in and I can now hear them,
a soft ripple in the air,
like afternoon humidity in the summer,
it's thick and inescapable.
I keep it together in the car ride home but then,
once I'm in the door,
in my room,
I release.
I begin to cry,
no,
to sob.
My parents sit either side of me,
sitting,
not hugging,
not comforting,
but sitting.
Listening while I exhaustedly weep,
and cough,
and pull myself together long enough to utter just one word—

'Why?'
This continues in an endless rolling cycle until,
firmly,
I am requested to stop crying,
to stop acting the way that I am,
to suppress,
to man up,
to just calm down,
to be … silent.
They leave and I …
and I suppress.
I don't know what else to do.

I'm about nineteen years old and I'm standing,
naked,
in an ankle-deep paddle pool,
in the backyard of my rental house.
It's around three in the morning and it's not exactly warm.
I'm shaking,
a mix of cold and adrenalin and something else.
Something I can't explain.
Something wordless,
known but unnamed.
My boyfriend,
at the time,
is standing in the doorway,
trying desperately to get me inside.
He is concerned but frustrated,
more frustrated but concerned.
He didn't sign up for this.
He just made one comment;
something he didn't think would cause this.
It was instant,
when he said it,
an instant reaction.
We were already in bed,
naked,

sleepy,
talking and then,
all the air sucked out from my lungs and I had to move.
To get away from him,
and somehow,
for some reason,
I ended up in the paddle pool,
water slick with sunscreen and body … fluids.
This was the only way I could express what I was feeling.
My head was foggy and I just reacted.
I was electrified and numb,
shaking but incredibly heavy.
I didn't know if this was the correct reaction,
the right reaction,
but it was all I could do.
I had to put what I was feeling somewhere,
make sense of the lightning going off through my body.
I couldn't talk,
couldn't cry,
couldn't control.
All I could do was stand and shake.
Stand naked in a grotty paddle pool,
staring into the night,
shaking,
uncontrollably.

I'm standing in the bathroom of my rented house.
I'm staring in the sink 'cause I don't actually know how I got here.
I've been awake for what seems like days not hours.
I am actually not even sure what day it is.
They have bled into one long cycle,
a repeated sunrise sunset pattern,
reliable but deceptive.
I smell,
standing here,
I can smell myself.
I haven't showered in days.

I haven't been in this room for a while.
The toilet is in the next room.
I have been there,
but just,
not in here.
I'm not doing well.
I'm not sure what exactly is happening.
I can't hold on to thoughts.
I can't think clearly.
I can't look in the mirror so I lean on the sink.
Shift my weight forward and stare.
There's a broken disposable razor in the sink.
I don't remember breaking it open.
I … I don't remember.

I'm eight years old and I am standing in front of my mother and I'm crying.
I was always a crying child.
I was until … I wasn't.
I don't know what I was crying about, but it was important.
I remember it being hard crying.
Painful.
Jabs in the lungs and tension in the jaw.
She was ironing and impatient.
She wouldn't even look at me.
It was as if she couldn't look at me.
Finally she put the iron down and glared,
eyes cutting through the blur of my tears.
'I guess tomorrow I should go down to the school and get you a dress to start wearing. Crying like that. Do you want me to do that? 'Cause if you keep on crying like this then that's what I'll do. If you don't stop crying that's what I'll do.'

I'm sitting on the balcony of my rented two-story unit,
staring into the night.
It's four in the morning and I can't sleep.
I'm drinking coffee,
black,

I can't afford milk,
and I'm smoking my second cigarette,
I budgeted for them.
I'm smoking slowly,
making them last.
I can hear the hum of the main road to my left.
There's always a hum.
I listen as I stare out,
into the black.
My cigarette is down to its last few puffs.
I take one slow long drag,
breathe deep and exhale.
I shift the butt in my finger,
turning it upside down,
and I put the cigarette out,
on the back of my left hand.
Squashing out the embers,
pressing deep into my charring flesh.
I honestly thought that I'd feel something.

I'm out and I'm dancing.
I'm overwhelmingly happy.
Everything in this moment has fallen into place.
Great music,
I am looking great,
out with some great friends,
and I can afford good booze.
It's a night for spirits and shots.
And I dance.
And I smile,
and I can't stop hugging people.
I'm tactile.
I'm hugging friends.
Holding their hands.
With permission,
because consent is sexy.
I chat to random people at the bar,

and tell strangers that they look great.
I smile,
big toothy grins,
the kind that are born from a giggle.
I kiss cheeks and fire off sly winks,
stroking faces and saying—
'I adore you', and meaning it.
I leave before things can take a downward spiral.
I walk home with pace,
breaking into a kind of run every once in a while.
The wind whips at my face,
and I close my eyes,
and then I'm home,
and I'm sitting on my bed,
and I'm buzzing,
and I'm shaking,
and I'm …

I'm sitting in a doctor's surgery,
sweating,
dry-mouthed.
He is waiting for me to speak and I … I …
'I think I need a mental health assessment 'cause I have started to look at how high buildings are and … '
He makes some notes on the computer and then turns to me and instantly I'm calmer.
He asks questions,
softly,
lightly,
but direct,
he wants answers,
and I am screaming at myself to not hold back.
Just answer the questions and answer openly and honestly.
Nothing is off-limits.
I don't know what the right words to use are,
but I know that I do not sound silly or emotional or overreacting …
and when I finish the words hang in the air like fog.

He makes more notes and then,
in his best opinion,
with the information given,
gives me a preliminary diagnosis and …
and then he passes me two things.
The details of a psychologist—
'Call him and keep calling until he answers.'
And a prescription—
'These are going to knock you around a bit, but we'll keep a close
    eye on you and see how you go.'
I thank him,
leave,
and sit on the tram,
and cry.
A beautiful movie moment really,
me looking out the window as the afternoon sun hits my face,
a single tear rolling down my cheek.
I cry with relief,
and pride,
and shame
… why did it take me this long to say something …

I am walking home from work and I am leaning too far to the right.
The pills I'm on make me feel like I am walking slightly slanted to
    the left,
which I'm not,
but because it's a very convincing feeling,
I compensate by leaning to the right,
which because I'm not actually leaning to the left,
means I am actually leaning to the right.
The doctor did say there would be side effects and when I picked up
    my first packet from the chemist,
I wait three days before I take my first pill and it fucks me up hard.
Everything feels like it's happening three seconds to the left.
I think I'm slurring my words,
which I'm not,
but I'm worried that I sound drunk at work.

I can't sleep from the vivid dreams and my sex drive increases,
which is quite rare as it usually goes the other way.
It wasn't a huge amount,
but I was definitely feeling myself a lot more.
This all lasted about two weeks and everyone kept asking if I felt any better …
but I didn't know how I should be feeling.
I'd never felt 'okay' so this new feeling,
this 'new normal' …
I was just as in the dark as everyone else.

It's Christmas and I am sitting on a stool in my parent's house.
I'm going over all my diagnoses and it's,
well it's not easier in person,
it's just …
what it is.
Dad's silent to my left and Mother is nodding along.
Nodding in agreement as each word is said,
out loud.
Nodding like she has always known.
Nodding like she has always known but did …
The nodding continues until I drop the big one.
Eyes widen,
Dad leaves,
and the nodding slows,
knowingly,
until I say—
'It can be hereditary or … '
Nodding turns into a shake and I'm silent.
I decide not to finish the sentence,
because the 'or' is that it could be the result of a traumatic childhood.
I decide it's best to keep that bit to myself …

I'm lying in bed and my mind still plays tricks on me.
The pills still make it hard to sleep,
and I just don't know if I should still be on them,
or if they are doing me more harm than good.
I don't know if I can even trust my own thoughts.

I think I'm getting better,
but what does that even mean?
I just keep thinking that maybe if I ... I ... I ... I ...

***

I feel like my hand has passed through to a second chamber,
an unexpected other place.
It was as if my fingers caressed the fleshy opening of a pipe,
a pipe that then gave way to an airy and surprisingly open space.
An open space inside someone.

I'm sweating,
a lot,
too much and all over.
I feel like I am slippery with sweat,
and lube,
and juices,
and ...

I didn't think that this situation would be so stressful.

Firstly, I had to really resist the urge to suddenly open my hand while inside him.
Once I was firmly forearm deep,
this impulse just seemed to come over me,
this little voice inside my head that started to whisper—
'Open your hand ... go on ... do it ... just quick ... go on ... just to see what would happen.'
Just to see what would happen?!
What would happen is that I would take out a kidney or some other part of his insides ...
I don't know how the human body works.

So while I'm trying not to think about that,
I suddenly remember that my housemate was coming back from their overseas vacation today,
but I couldn't remember whether they were arriving back to the house in the daytime or in the evening,
and normally I wouldn't care,

but I seem to have left my bedroom door wide open,
and my naked ass is up,
and splayed for everyone to see.
Now I'm not to concerned with them seeing my naked ass,
'cause squats,
but I just know that they'll stand there,
in the doorway to my room,
giggle,
and then take out their phone,
and … click … click … click … click …

I started to feel really trapped.
Sweat beading across my forehead and …
is that my fingers?
I had moved my hand,
slightly,
and across the guy's stomach I saw;
at least I think I saw,
a flash of my own fingers.
No,
can't be.
But I decide to do a little experiment.
I slowly,
carefully,
ever so slightly,
curled my fingers towards me and …
oh yep …
that is indeed my fingers sliding across the inside of his stomach.

You know what,
I think I'm done.
I think I have definitely learnt a lot about myself and about my
    limits and I would like to—
'More, more!' he pants,
before reaching down,
grabbing my forearm with both hands,
and pulling himself further down,
and my arm further in …

It was …
and I felt …

I felt like I was going to …

***

I'm standing in my mate's kitchen,
sculling the last of my drink.
The car has arrived and we are rushing to get out the door.
I finish,
Burp,
and then,
unexpectedly,
begin to vomit.
Hard.
This full-forced stream of vomit splashing down onto the kitchen floor.
And it was as if I had become hyperaware of what was happening.
My mate,
the one whose house it was,
was just staring at me.
Blankly staring.
My other friend,
to my left,
just kept yelling—
'You're vomiting on the floor.'
Thank you,
I am well aware.
When I finally stopped,
I wiped my mouth,
spat the last of the muck onto the floor,
and we left.
In the car my mate shrugged and said—
'I'll clean it up when I get back.'

It's four a.m. and I am leaving a newly acquired friend's house.
He lives on the top of a high hill.
Not a mountain as such but there is definitely some altitude to the
    surrounds.

The driver isn't driving particularly fast,
nor is the street that winding,
but I have had a lot to drink,
and I can start to feel the spit in my mouth building.
That telltale sign that you have a very limited amount of time to find a toilet,
or shrub,
or back alley,
before all hell breaks loose.
But it was rapidly becoming a hopeless situation.
Knowing that the purge was imminent I had a brainwave.
A stroke of genius.
I opened the sleeve of my jacket and as the bile rose,
I sank my mouth further in and vomited all down my arm,
feeling the warmth as it began to pool in the elbow of my jacket.
Dignity intact,
I strutted from the car,
into my motel room,
and hurled the jacket into the shower,
turning the tap on full,
before collapsing onto the bed as the stench of moist vomit filled the room.

I wake up to a blinding hangover and my housemate screaming at me to get in the car.
We work together and,
well she's actually my manager,
and today is going to be busy,
and I am running late.
I get to the bathroom,
sink-wash my junk,
and make it to the car in about ten minutes flat.
The car ride to work is agony.
My head is swirling,
my breathing is laboured,
and I stink.
My pores are spilling out the remnants of the night before.

We park a few blocks from work 'cause it's a Sunday,
and she's walking front of me,
striding out in front,
angry,
really pissed off.
'You know, I don't actually feel too bad ... '
I didn't get to finish the end of that sentence,
'cause suddenly,
but not unexpectedly,
this hot stream of bright orange vomit hurls itself out of my mouth
    and begins to pool at my feet.
And there is just so much of it.
My feet are sopping and the heat.
I could feel the heat through my shoes.
The stream seemed to last what felt like a full minute,
maybe even two,
when finally it finishes,
and my housemate says, 'Better?'
in a really patronising tone.
'Much' I smirk back.
That was a very tense day at work.

I'm at university,
it's Uni Night and I am drinking two-dollar boxed wine and juice.
Yum.
I'm on the dance floor and a friend asks if I want another round.
'Give me sec,' I say and head to the bathroom.
I walk straight into the cubicle,
kneel down,
and licking my fingers so that they will slide down with ease.
It doesn't take me long and I am bringing back up my dinner,
my pre-drinks,
and the drinks I had already drunk earlier that night.
All the while my right knee was becoming sopped with urine that
    had collected next to the seat,
and my fingers were becoming streaked with blood from slamming
    them down my throat.

Once I am done,
I wash my face,
spit in the sink,
and head to the bar.
I throw down ten dollars and wait as they line up five drinks.
I scull three,
pick up the remaining two,
and rejoin my friends on the dance floor.

I am waking up and something feels,
wrong.
I'm twisted up in my sheets but I'm …
I'm still wearing my clothes …
and well,
I'm wearing half my clothes.
I'm half-undressed.
And not the half you might think.
Not top or bottom half, no, no,
I'm mean half like straight down the middle.
Somehow when I was getting into bed,
I undressed just one arm and just one leg.
Like jumper,
shirt,
pants,
even underwear,
all half off and no idea how or why I did it.
How is that even comfortable?

I wake up with a jolt and a stab of pain through my temple.
It takes me longer than it should to realise that I am in my own bed.
I stay there for most of the day,
blinds drawn,
movement to a minimum.
When I finally venture outside for food I notice I still have my cab-fair money in my wallet.
A quick call on my phone establishes that no transaction has been made that would equal a taxi payment …
but I know I was in one.

I know that I caught a cab home.
I remember being in the front seat and the driver ...
and the ...
How did I pay for the cab?

I'm in Greece with a friend and we are at a bar called The Shamrock Fun Club.
Heaven.
It's the kind of place that has everything, literally—
there's a pool table,
and a big-screen TV,
and a dance floor,
and a pole, for pole dancing.
Cheap cocktails and hot waiters.
We make friends with the owner and stay drinking well after it's closed.
When we finally leave, the hot waiters walk with us a little of the way and then turn off to head to wherever it is they are going.
I'm not done though,
and in my blurry drunk haze I run,
run after the boys through the winding back streets of Corfu.
I find them,
somehow,
and giggle and drooling my words as I wrap my arms round them.
They seem happy to see me but they do slowly and purposefully lead me back to my hotel.
I stumble up the stairs and into the room,
my friend is still on the bed and she's been crying.
'I didn't know where you went'—
She said with a calm firmness.
'You ran off and I didn't know where you were. If something happened, if something happened to you, how do I even begin to find you?'

I can feel the heat of the sun against the train window as I slowly peel my face from it.
I've drooled down my face and onto my shirt.
There's a streak of sweat across the window and my hat has fallen onto the floor.

I am surprisingly pulling into my stop when I realise that …
it's daytime.
It shouldn't be daytime.
I got on the train at night-time,
Well four in the morning,
but still essentially,
night-time.
I can remember dancing at a club.
I remember a guy telling me I was adorable.
I remember him saying that he wasn't interested in dating 'cause he just came out of a pretty fucked-up relationship.
I remember getting aggressive and spitting my drink in his face.
I remember walking,
stumbling to the train station.
I remember sitting at the window,
leaning my head against the glass and then …
that train goes to the mountains and back …
I was on that train for six hours …

I stare at my phone and it is heavy with messages …
some are funny …
most are rejecting my sexual advances …
a lot are calling me out on my behaviour,
and there's one that's asking if I'm okay.
Why? …
''Cause you ran out in front of four lanes of traffic last night, for no reason and I wanted to make sure you were okay.'

I am two drinks in and I am feeling … smooth.
Everything is better once I'm two drinks in.
That's all it takes.
Two drinks for the limbs to feel looser.
Two drinks for the wine to taste better.
Two drinks for the cigarettes to catch less in the back of the throat.
Two drinks for the wit to be wittier,
the sass to be sassier,
and the inhibitions to just fall away.
Two drinks in and I want more.

Two drinks starts the night,
means it'll be a good night,
means the night never has to end.
Two drinks in and I'm day-drinking,
letting the afternoon heat brush my face.
Two drinks in and I am in for the long haul.
Two drinks in and I am the life of the party.
Two drinks in and I can't stop.
Two drinks in and I won't stop.

I am two bottles of wine in and I'm … crying.
I've been crying for the last three hours and I just don't know why.
My head hurts,
swirling,
rapidly,
and I can barely grab on to anything.
I feel giddy,
and off-balance,
and my jaw has locked from crying.
I text a friend …
and say that I am in a bad way and I need …
and they say—
'Yeah nights like that are shit,
but you'll get through it …
you'll be fine in the morning.'

I am,
today—
    Count from the 22nd October 2018.
days sober.
I am (X) days sober and I feel … awful.
If anyone who's stopped drinking tells you that they feel great,
and it's just a blast … they are lying.
They are dirty fucking liars,
'cause it is horrid.
It is just the worst.

I am (X) days sober and I am irritated by everything ...
and everyone.
Some people just won't stop talking.
Everything I used to find tolerable has just gone out the window.
Now even the slightest inconvenience sets me off and I am ready to go.
I am a fiery boiling pot of rage just bubbling to explode.

I am (X) days sober and I am so bored.
It's as if my capacity to care has been dialled down to like a two ...
it's like I'm just coasting through life with not a care in the world ...
not a care about anything.
And I bore myself the most.
I used to be the fun one,
a fun drunk but now ...
It feels like there is a part of me that's missing.
That thing that made social situations bearable,
that made me bearable.

I am (X) days sober and I don't know what to do with my hands,
or with a lot of my limbs for that matter.
I don't know how to dance anymore,
I don't dance anymore.
I loved to dance,
the freedom of it was ...
intoxicating ...
but now I feel very seen,
exposed,
uncomfortable ...
it's like I know I'm about to do something wrong,
and everyone will see ...
everyone.

I am (X) days sober and everyone wants me to be their inspiration,
their guide,
their sobriety Sherpa,
if you will.
And you know what,

no,
I'm busy.
I am busy trying,
trying to keep myself afloat.
You want an inspirational quote?
'Go sort out your own life and leave me alone!'

I am (X) days sober and when the pandemic hit,
when we had to go into lockdown,
and everyone was plunged into a world of uncertainty,
I actually had a few friends,
on numerous occasions,
say to me—
'Well this will really test your sobriety, hey?'
Not helpful!

I am (X) days sober and I am terrified.
I had a dream recently,
one of those incredibly vivid dreams,
the kind where everything feels ... real.
So in the dream I'm out with friends,
I can't see who they are but we are having fun.
The music is loud,
and the lights flicker across my gaze,
and a nondescript friend has a glass of wine in their hand.
White.
Crisp.
Chilled.
Without hesitation,
I reach out and take a sip.
One sip.
And then I have another.
And then I have a glass.
And then I have two more.
And then,
dream me is cackling with laughter and saying—
'Well, I guess I drink now.'
I woke up in mid-panic attack,

trying to remember if it actually happened.
I sat on the edge of my bed shaking,
going over every moment that I could remember,
trying to see if what I was feeling was real.
I sat there all morning,
utterly exhausted,
and totally terrified.
'Cause that's all it would take,
for all this to unravel,
one sip …
just one sip.

I am (X) days sober and I don't need alcohol to get through my day …
but I want it.

I think what I loathe most in the world,
is hindsight.
Like if I met hindsight down a dark alleyway,
things would not end well.
I can't help but think,
what if?
What if things had been different,
if I had been different?
What if I had just talked more?
What if I just knew the words to say?
What if I had been listened to?

Everything changed for me when I learnt my words,
the words that don't define me,
but do help to explain …
me.
Why I didn't know them sooner I will never know,
but I know them now,
and I am going to scream them from the rooftops.

So with that in mind,
I want to share with you,

my words.
Out loud.
To shatter this silence …

My words are:
severe anxiety,
clinical depression,
suicidal tendencies,
borderline personality disorder,
and alcohol abuse.

I'm an alcoholic.

And when you leave here,
I want you to take a moment and think,
what are yours?

***

WAIT!

Sweat dripping down my brow,
breathing shallow and laboured,
arm shaking inside …
someone …
I'm ready to concede defeat and negotiate the removal of my arm,
when all of a sudden his phone beeps.
He reaches over,
checks it,
types back a message,
turns to me and says—
'I should go, I'm late for a first date.'
He then places a foot either side of my forearm,
and slooses himself off,
gets dressed and leaves.

He was fired,
fisted,
and first-dated,
all on the same day.

And to this day,
when the wind blows just right,
I still get a phantom fisting feeling,
running down my arm.

THE END

GAVIN ROACH

presents

YOUR SILENCE WILL NOT PROTECT YOU

(PART 3 OF THE ANXIETY TRILOGY)

13–17 SEPTEMBER, 2022

Writer and Performer
Gavin Roach

Director
Lauren Hopley

PLAYWRIGHT'S NOTE

I was told that I was too angry. That I needed to let it go. That was where it all began. An acquaintance at a dinner party telling me that I was holding onto the past and it was causing me harm. My response … I told them to fuck off. And then I wrote. I wrote what I always thought would be the second story, but it became the first, (the second proved way too complex and I'm a lazy writer, so I often take the easy way out.)

It wasn't a planned trilogy; there was a definite plan for more than one story but not necessarily three connected works. But, as often happens, I tried to fit too much in one work and it spilled over into the next and then into the next and eight years later, *The Anxiety Trilogy* comes full circle.

Each story proved to be wrought with its own unique challenge—from panic attacks, to cancelled seasons, to on-stage blackouts and lines that wouldn't stick, (which meant that I just made it up on the spot night after night.) Sometimes I would stand offstage and think, 'Why do you have to do this?' I mean, I didn't HAVE to, no-one forced me, but I wanted to tell these stories.

And they took me further than I ever thought I would go, both as a performer and on a personal level. I got to stand on stages in places that I never thought I'd stand on, sharing stories with strangers (and the Irish Prime Minister … seriously) that I never thought I'd meet. And all while working out some deep-seeded issues.

I never wanted to make 'therapy on stage' works but I did, but more for me than any expectation placed on the audience to work out the inner functions of my psyche … (I pay a lovely therapist for that.) I always hope that there is something in each work that audiences connect with, something that maybe they can relate to and will help in some way. Or maybe I have just made three works that entertain … fingers crossed.

I haven't performed or written work for myself to perform since writing and performing these works, and maybe I won't, maybe for now, this is it, and if so, well then I'm pretty damn proud.

—**Gavin Roach**
July 2022

DIRECTOR'S NOTE

Gav and I first met at uni in country NSW. He was in his third year, and I was in my first, and while we moved in the same broad circle of acting students it wasn't until years later, when we both returned to the same uni to undertake our Honours year, that we became close. Both originally from Sydney, we had moved to what felt like another world to study acting and directing, and the opportunities that being away from home offered up allowed us to begin our adult lives with a special kind of freedom and energy. Fast forward a decade and a half, and Gav and I are still channeling that feeling, finding creative ways to express who we are. Part of that journey for Gav has been writing and performing *The Anxiety Trilogy*, and it has been my privilege to work alongside my dear friend in directing these plays and helping him bring his words to life.

The Anxiety Trilogy is a testament to the courage of exploring what shapes us, even when it hurts; especially when it hurts. In the rehearsal period for *I Can't Say the F Word*, I learned about the moments that chipped away at my friend when he was young, cuts and slices that have shaped the Gavin I know today. *F Word* was first staged in a little theatre/art gallery in Richmond, Melbourne: an intimate space to watch the vulnerability of Gav's writing evolve into a heartfelt performative exploration of his experiences with bullying and homophobia.

The Measure of a Man took that vulnerability a step further, seeing Gav lay bare his sexual anxieties for an audience up close. Gav and I were both flat out with another play we were staging at the time and had a frantic six days after closing the first play to get *Measure* on its feet. Not only did we succeed, but Gav has since travelled both nationally and internationally to perform this gem of a show.

When Gav pitched me the concept for *Your Silence Will Not Protect You*, I felt simultaneously nervous and excited for him to undertake this final exploration of self in the series. Delving into the deeply personal and raw subject matter of alcoholism and mental illness, Gav found the right note to round out the *Trilogy*, and his bravery and commitment to leave it all on the stage always makes me smile.

I hope you enjoy the ride, dear audience. It's bumpy and beautiful, as all the best adventures are.

—Lauren Hopley
July 2022

GAVIN ROACH
WRITER / PERFORMER

Gavin Roach has a Bachelor of Arts (Acting for the Screen and Stage), Bachelor of Arts (Acting for the Screen and Stage, Honours) CSU, Masters in Arts Management, UTS, and Masters in Writing for Performance, VCA.

Gavin is the writer, performer and producer of *Confessions of a Grindr Addict* (Sydney, Melbourne, Newcastle, Edinburgh, Perth, Adelaide, Launceston, Hobart and New Zealand), *Any Womb Will Do* (Sydney, Melbourne and New Zealand), *I Can't Say The F Word* (Melbourne, Perth and New Zealand), *The Measure of a Man* (Melbourne, Sydney, Perth, Hobart, Brisbane, Prague and Dublin), *All The Songs I Can't Sing* (Melbourne) and *Your Silence Will Not Protect You* (Melbourne).

Gavin adapted and produced *Beyond Priscilla: The Play* and was the co-devisor and co-creative developer of *We Were There*, showcasing the stories of women during the HIV/AIDS crisis in Australia.

Gavin's producing credits include *Manwatching*, *All I See Is You*, *The Loneliness Project*, *Adam*, *The Campaign*, *Sink*, *Transgression*, and *Meet Me at Dawn*. Gavin has produced and directed *Lake Disappointment*, *Awkward Conversations With Animals I've Fucked*, *The Shy Manifesto*, *Run*, *Bottom*, and *A Hundred Words For Snow*.

LAUREN HOPLEY
DIRECTOR

Lauren Hopley has been making theatre in Melbourne and across Australia for the past 15 years. She has directed, acted and written for companies and organisations including National Trust of Australia, Corner Boy Productions, Driven Outcomes, TIE: Quality theatre in Education, Class Act Theatre Company, Wooden Leg Theatre Company, Gearstick Productions, Karrikins Group, CSU University Theatre Ensemble, and the University of Montana, USA. She has a Bachelor of Arts in Acting, an Honours degree in Directing, and an Executive Master of Arts degree.

Since 2014, Lauren has collaborated with playwright Gavin Roach to put LGBTI stories up in lights, having directed part one of *The Anxiety Trilogy*, *I Can't Say The F Word*, for Melbourne Fringe in 2014, and two plays, *Beyond Priscilla: The Play* and part two of *The Anxiety Trilogy*, *Measure of A Man*, for Midsumma 2016. Part three of *The Anxiety Trilogy*, *Your Silence Will Not Protect You*, was staged in 2019.

Audience interactivity, bold characters, and a landscape of actual events are a common canvas for her work.

www.currency.com.au

Visit Currency Press' website now to:

- Order books
- Browse through our full list of titles including plays, screenplays, theory and reference/criticism, performance handbooks, educational texts and more
- Choose a play for your school or performance group by cast specs
- Seek performance rights
- Find out about performing arts news and sign up for our newsletter
- For students: read our study guides
- For teachers: access free curriculum information and teacher notes

We are also on Facebook and Instagram (@currencypress). Join the conversation!

The performing arts publisher

LAUREN HOPLEY
DIRECTOR

Lauren Hopley has been making theatre in Melbourne and across Australia for the past 15 years. She has directed, acted and written for companies and organisations including National Trust of Australia, Corner Boy Productions, Driven Outcomes, TIE: Quality theatre in Education, Class Act Theatre Company, Wooden Leg Theatre Company, Gearstick Productions, Karrikins Group, CSU University Theatre Ensemble, and the University of Montana, USA. She has a Bachelor of Arts in Acting, an Honours degree in Directing, and an Executive Master of Arts degree.

Since 2014, Lauren has collaborated with playwright Gavin Roach to put LGBTI stories up in lights, having directed part one of *The Anxiety Trilogy*, *I Can't Say The F Word*, for Melbourne Fringe in 2014, and two plays, *Beyond Priscilla: The Play* and part two of *The Anxiety Trilogy*, *Measure of A Man*, for Midsumma 2016. Part three of *The Anxiety Trilogy*, *Your Silence Will Not Protect You*, was staged in 2019.

Audience interactivity, bold characters, and a landscape of actual events are a common canvas for her work.

development of production-specific surround systems to accommodate his theatrical and sound art designs. Connor's theatrical work has extended from engineering and systems design, sound effects and foley, through to fully scored productions and the development of new musicals. Connor's theatrical scores are heavily based on the idea of recurring motifs to reinforce thematic elements of a text, subtly influencing an audience throughout a work.

Recent theatrical credits include work on: *Kerosene* at Theatre Works (Dir. Benjamin Nichol, 2021); *Lobby Hero* at fortyfivedownstairs (Dir. James Vinson, Around the Moon Productions, 2019); *Lake Disappointment* at Meat Market (Dir. Gavin Roach, Melbourne Fringe, 2019); *My Wife Peggy* at Gasworks Arts Park (Dir. Gavin Roach, Gasworks Premiere, 2019); *We Were There* at Chapel Off Chapel (Dir. Dirk Hoult, Tilted Projects, 2018); *Macbeth* at Southbank Theatre (Dir. Simon Phillips, Melbourne Theatre Company, 2017).

Connor's sound art practice has a particular focus on how the sounds within natural environments organically mix, and how created and composed elements can be introduced to this mix. His ongoing body of work *Spaces In Between* explores this concept and has so far involved the taking of field recordings at a number of significant National Parks sites across Victoria. The work was first presented as part of RMIT's *SIAL Studios Ambisonic Modelling Concert* in 2017 and was then commissioned for a re-development by City of Melbourne for the Signal Sound Commissions in 2019. In 2021 Connor undertook a residency at the Bogong Centre for Sound Culture to further develop the project, and has since shown further developments at Testing Grounds.

DALLAS PALMER
GEORGE

Dallas is a Melbourne-based actor. Since graduating with a BA in Musical Theatre from BAPA in 2004 he has gone on to work and train with some of the world's most renowned teachers and practitioners. Dallas was selected to work with Ivana Chubbuck in her 2010 masterclass here in Melbourne which subsequently lead to working with her personally for five months at her private studio based in Hollywood.

A graduate of the full-time course at 16th St Actors Studio in Melbourne in 2013, he went on to work with many master teachers and coaches including NYC Actors Studio Elizabeth Kemp in 2014, Larry Moss, Carol Rosenfeld from NYC HB Studios and in 2017 spent two weeks working and training with British theatre legend Mike Alfred.

Theatre credits include *My Wife Peggy* (Gasworks Theatre, Melbourne, 2019), *And the Snow Fell on Egypt* (Midsummer Festival, 2019) Stephen Sondheim's *Company* (Dir: Tom Healy), *Journey's End* (New Theatre, Sydney) *Vieux Carre* by Tennessee Williams (Itch Productions at fortyfivedownstairs) and *This Is What It Feels Like* (La Mama). Feature films include *Mortal Foods* (Phil Moore), *Moonlight and Magic* (Timothy Burns), and *Mormon Yankees—The Spirt of the Game* (Dir: Darren Page).

CONNOR ROSS
SOUND DESIGNER

Connor Ross is a sound designer and composer who focuses on creating immersive auditory environments for theatre, screen, installations and sound art projects. He has a particular focus on using organic, ambient textures to develop mood and tension in his work. With a background and ongoing career as a live sound engineer, Connor utilizes this experience in his

GAVIN ROACH
WRITER / DIRECTOR

Gavin Roach has a Bachelor of Arts (Acting for the Screen and Stage), Bachelor of Arts (Acting for the Screen and Stage, Honours) CSU, Masters in Arts Management, UTS, and Masters in Writing for Performance, VCA.

Gavin is the writer, performer and producer of *Confessions of a Grindr Addict* (Sydney, Melbourne, Newcastle, Edinburgh, Perth, Adelaide, Launceston, Hobart and New Zealand), *Any Womb Will Do* (Sydney, Melbourne and New Zealand), *I Can't Say The F Word* (Melbourne, Perth and New Zealand), *The Measure of a Man* (Melbourne, Sydney, Perth, Hobart, Brisbane, Prague and Dublin), *All The Songs I Can't Sing* (Melbourne) and *Your Silence Will Not Protect You* (Melbourne).

Gavin adapted and produced *Beyond Priscilla: The Play* and was the co-devisor and co-creative developer of *We Were There*, showcasing the stories of women during the HIV/AIDS crisis in Australia.

Gavin's producing credits include *Manwatching*, *All I See Is You*, *The Loneliness Project*, *Adam*, *The Campaign*, *Sink*, *Transgression*, and *Meet Me at Dawn*. Gavin has produced and directed *Lake Disappointment*, *Awkward Conversations With Animals I've Fucked*, *The Shy Manifesto*, *Run*, *Bottom*, and *A Hundred Words For Snow*.

ACTOR'S NOTE

Gavin and I first presented *My Wife Peggy* as part of Gasworks Arts Park's play reading sessions in September 2018. The first time I read this play I knew in my gut that there was life in it and I knew that I wanted to be the person to bring George to the stage. So to hear after that first public reading that Gasworks wanted to pick it up for a season as part of their Premier season in 2019, I was totally ecstatic that this beautiful and heartbreaking new work would be given the opportunity to breathe new life on stage.

When you work in independent theatre, the creative process and exploration of a project can often be pushed aside for myriad reasons. Time constraints, money, budget, funding, availability of arts spaces ... I'll stop myself there but I could go on. So we were both thrilled when we were given a year to develop *Peggy* from the ground up.

As an actor, the creative process and gift of time to bring something new to life is paramount and something I always approach with great respect and curiosity. To be given the space to explore George's world was a beautifully poignant and often terrifying experience for me ... to navigate and explore a world which we all know but very rarely like to face.

I want to say grief but I won't. Because to me grief comes later on in the process.

What *My Wife Peggy* is more interested in is (for me at least) looking at what happens in those initial moments after immediate loss. When in a mere matter of moments a life has been completely and utterly transformed. A life that will never be the same again. That delicate dance between denial and shock, fear and rage, sadness and humour, and love and anger. When a human's world is irrevocably changed, how would one be in that space and time?

It's not an easy subject or topic to work with but over time it revealed a heartwarming beauty whilst also being profoundly dark and honest.

It has been an absolute joy to work with Gavin on *My Wife Peggy* and I'm indebted to him for trusting me with such beautiful and heartfelt material. To be able to continue on with even more curiosity and desire to see how it will evolve is a blessing and I couldn't be more excited to bring it to a wider audience.

—**Dallas Palmer**
May 2021

PLAYWRIGHT'S NOTE

The spark that inspired *My Wife Peggy* came from my dad.

I had moved back into my childhood home and not long after I did, my mother went into hospital for a knee reconstruction. A fairly routine surgery with very few risks. The night before her surgery, it was just my dad and I at home and he could not and would not sit still. He was a ball of bottled-up anxiety, worryingly pacing from room to room and rather firmly stating, 'Your mother's not going to make it.' (Much like myself, my dad has a flair for the dramatic.)

My mother was fine, by the way. Everything went well and she was back on her feet in no time, but looking back, what I insensitively brushed off was not my dad's long-term grief at a life without my mother but rather he was afraid of the beginning. That overwhelming 'what do I do now ... right now,' when you are confronted with loss. I didn't know it at the time but it was at that moment that *My Wife Peggy* was born.

Step by step and little by little the character of George, the story's central character, formed. With the help of my Masters of Writing for Performance at VCA cohort, this scattered collection of unconnected vignettes (which I called vinaigrettes, without a hint of irony, for far too long) soon morphed into the play you are about to see (or have seen or read, if you just bought the script).

More than a lot of my other characters, I have a real soft spot for George. He is at the edge of a very high cliff and the only way is down, into the unknown. He's scared and alone and for the first time in a long time, without a lifeline. He knows he can't stay still for long but he just can't bring himself to move. I've tried to be kind to him without compromising the story too much.

My Wife Peggy was first staged as part of Premiere at Gasworks Arts Park, a program to assist independent Melbourne-based artists and creatives to stage original productions. I am incredibly grateful for all of the support and guidance Gasworks Arts Park has given me—not just in getting this work to the stage but throughout the early stages of my artistic development.

I never really thought that this work would ever get to the stage but gosh I'm so very grateful that it has. I didn't do it alone though— Dallas Palmer, Connor Ross and Clare Springette all contributed their incredible artistic talents and elevated the work to what it is today.

—**Gavin Roach**
May 2021

GAVIN ROACH

presents

MY WIFE PEGGY

13–17 SEPTEMBER, 2022

Writer
Gavin Roach

Director
Gavin Roach

Sound Designer
Connor Ross

Lighting Designer
Clare Springett

George
Dallas Palmer

MY WIFE PEGGY

Scream 'Daddy' and throw themselves at me while I fall on the
   couch.
We'll fall just as you sit up;
arms outstretched
and we'll all end up in a heap.
Laughing.
Laughing at each other.
Laughing together.
You and me tickling them girls,
as they wriggle around in fits of giggles.
Remember how we used to do that Peg?
Let's go do that now.
Just get up
and we'll go jump on the girls.
They won't care.
We'll give them the day off school
and we can sit up all night watching TV,
finishing off the birthday cake.
You'll have to make room on the couch though Peg.
So you gotta get up now hey.
Come on get up Peg.
Get up.
Get up Peg.
Come on.
Get up, hey.
Get …

    Snap to blackout.

THE END

The girls are going to wake up soon,
so sit up yeah.
Damn it, Peg.
Stop ignoring me.
Just for once in your goddamn life do as you're told
and sit the fuck up.
Sit up and talk to me Peg.
Ask me how my day was.
Do you wanna know how my day was?
Even if you're only half listening,
just sit up and ask.
There's not much to say Peg,
'bout my day,
but I like telling you.
I'd tell you anything.
So you gotta listen.
I mean it's just polite.
You're being really rude Peg,
shutting me out.
Laying there,
ignoring me.
You're probably having a good laugh at me.
Holding your lips tight together so you don't burst.
Well just let it out, Peg.
Just laugh at me.
Come on Peg.
Laugh hey?
Laugh at me and then don't stop.
Just laugh
and laugh
and laugh
and when you don't think you can,
just try and laugh some more,
'cause joke's on me, right.
You're going to get up
and tell me that this was all just one big fucking joke.
You going to get the girls to run out as well?

MY WIFE PEGGY

Buy new jeans.
Paint the lounge room.
Turn the TV off.
Listen to the girls,
Read more.
Books not magazines.
Play a sport.
I should get back into playing footy again.
Try gardening.
Stop crying.
Stop grieving.
Get a hobby.
Get a puppy.
Clean up after the puppy.
Should have gotten a kitten instead.
Never have this kind of trouble with a cat.
Christ, Peg, how many times do I have to say it?
We aren't getting a bloody kitten.
You know you're going to have to answer me at some stage.
Even just to shut me up.
You know how I hate silences?
Maybe you could sit up and ask me about my day, hey?
We didn't get to do that yesterday.
You were making dinner
and the girls wanted all my attention
and you know what I'm like with those two.
They just gotta look at me with those little eyes
and I'm done.
I give in every time.

So, how was my day then?
Come on Peg.
You gotta sit up for this.
Sit up Peg.
Hey come on Peg.
Sit up.
Throw the blanket off and sit up.

Is there a build up and then,
you realise that you're dying.
Or dead?
Was it like when a fever breaks?
There's all that pressure and then,
like a bubble bursting inside you,
you feel that tingle of relief take over.
Was it like that, Peg?
Was it like that?

I suppose I should call someone.
An ambulance or the police or …
But, I mean, you're dead.
Cold.
There's no coming back from where you are.
But someone's gotta come and take you away.
Look after the …
We didn't really discuss this, did we Peg?
What we wanted done when we died.
I don't know if you wanted to be buried or cremated.
I'm going to have you buried,
just so you know.
There's no way I'm going to let them burn you.
I don't care if that's what you wanted,
it's not going to happen Peg.
I couldn't have you trapped in a jar,
sitting on the shelf there,
looking at me.
Watching over me.
Telling me to get on with my life.
Raise the girls better.
Eat better.
Drink less.
Get more sleep.
Move on.
Find someone new.
Try yoga.

MY WIFE PEGGY

Telling me to get off my arse and move your body.
What's it like then hey?
Heaven?
Is it everything we were told?
Is it paradise, Peg?
Should I find out for myself?
Just run a bath,
grab the toaster
and wake up on a cloud,
you wrapped in my arms.
Sounds pretty good hey, Peg?
Yeah sounds like a pretty damn good idea to me.
Maybe that's the answer then hey?
Just not give a fuck about anyone else
and join you up there in paradise.

Or did it all just go black?
Are we all just kidding ourselves,
thinking that there is something waiting for us at the end?
Wouldn't that be a kick in the guts, hey?
Work our whole lives,
try as hard as we can to be good people,
thinking that there's something waiting for us at the end.
Only to find out that there's nothing.
Nothing at all.
Did you just close your eyes and …
Did you feel any pain?
Shit, did it hurt?
Dying?
Does it hurt?
Going the way you did.
I mean I imagine that getting hit by a bus
or getting stabbed would be a bloody painful way to go,
but this way,
your way,
just closing your eyes.
Does that hurt?

She can't stay alive for just one more birthday
but she knows a goddamn dead language.

We stand
and then sit
and then stand again
and I just follow blindly along.
I say the amen bits though,
them bits I know,
and after a while,
I kinda get into it.
She still hasn't said a word to me,
till finally it ends
and we head to the car.
We get in and start driving and next thing,
she starts talking about Christmas Day
and what needs to be done,
and who's bringing what
and what time we have to get up in the morning
and I'm just nodding along like we weren't just in church for the
    last two fucking hours.

After that night, there's no mention of church or nothing
till the next Christmas when we do it all again.

And then, one day,
out of nowhere,
she says she wants to go on a holiday,
a pilgrimage,
to Rome.
Not Italy.
Rome.
'It's calling me,' she says,
and I say, 'Well let's do it then.'
Never seemed to get around to making it happen though, did we?

So, where did you end up then, hey?
You up there looking down at me?

MY WIFE PEGGY

So, we're having it out and the whole time she's kinda edging me
    to the bedroom,
slowly manoeuvring me this way and that
and next thing,
I'm standing at the foot of the bed,
looking at the clothes she's bloody laid out for me.

Fuck you're good.

Well of course I got dressed,
she waited,
in the car,
and off we went to midnight mass.
We didn't say a word the whole trip,
except for when Peg needed to tell me which way to go,
cause I had no fucking idea.

We get there and it's like something out of the twilight zone.
Never seen the show myself,
just know the quote.
So, we go in and it's silent,
like dead silent.
Ha, dead silent.
We take our seats and Peg is straight into it.
Hands clasped tight, head bowed
and she is muttering some prayer I could barely make out.
I look around and everyone else is doing the same
and I start looking for the exits
'cause if this is one of them fucking churches were they start
    speaking in tongues, then I'm out.
I'm so fucking out.

So the priest or whatever gets up and starts talking
and I have no idea what he's saying,
but everyone else seems to be following him perfectly.
Later, she tells me that the whole thing was in Latin.
Latin.

gets to pick and choose, this one does.
Anyway, it was Christmas Eve and I'm watching TV,
something mindless,
more staring than watching,
and next thing,
out comes Peggy all dressed up looking like the bride of Christ.
Bride of Frankenstein more like.

She'll hate I said that,
should get a reaction out of her.

So, she's standing there and I,
well I just burst out laughing, don't I?
I mean you have to though.
There she is, not said a word about it all day,
standing there looking like it's Halloween,
and she expects me not to laugh.
Oh, and didn't she give me a glare.
At least I think she did,
was a bit hard to see your eyes through that heavy veil she had on.

She says we gotta get up and go to mass
and I just keep on fucking laughing cause this is the first I'm hearing
    of it.
She has NEVER mentioned nothing 'bout religion or God or
    nothing up until now
and I think she is having me on,
and she's still staring, probably.
So I ask what she's playing at
and she just says it again,
'We gotta get up and go to mass.'
I tell her I'm not going,
still having a laugh and then,
fuck do we have it out.
She starts yelling and I burr up and give it to her back.
Christ, I'm going to miss our scraps.

MY WIFE PEGGY

Well then Peg, your turn.
I have a fair idea that you got mixed up with a few guys behind me
     back.
How many?
Do I know 'em?
Yeah I bet I do, hey.
Yeah, you're just the sort to get it on with one of my mates.
And what about the girls then?
They even mine?
Cause there were times when I thought that maybe …
sometimes I catch myself looking at them and thinking,
'They don't look like me, not really.'
I can see you in them,
they have your smirk
and especially that little one,
she has your ears.
And they both have your eyes, Peg.
Fuck me, how am I supposed to look at them now, hey?
Every time I look them in the eye
I'm going to keep on seeing you.
Do you know how fucking hard that's going to be, Peg?
Well?

Bloody hell,
I'm sorry, Peg.
I'm sorry.
I'm sorry.

We were meant to go to Rome, you and me.
She's obsessed with the place.
Not Italy.
Rome.
There's a difference, apparently.
She has this latent Catholic streak in her that comes out when it
     suits her.
First time she sprung it on me was our first Christmas living together.
Living in sin, mind you,
but that's where the latent bit comes in,

Dance with me Peg,
just this one last time.

> GEORGE *starts slowly dancing, humming Sade's 'Smooth
> Operator'.*

Remember that night?
We would have been dating for a few months
and this song came on
and I said that I loved Sadie
and you just, you just burst out laughing
and I had no idea what you were laughing at
and you just kept on laughing.
Big belly laughs that made you catch your breath
and I, I just started laughing too cause,
fucking hell Peg, when you laugh.

Took you ages to calm down and finally tell me that it is pronounced
    Sade,
and I felt like an idiot
but you must have seen the look on my face,
cause you grabbed me,
pulled me in tight
and kissed me.

God, I need you to kiss me again, Peg.

Ever fool round on me then?
You can tell me, cause lord knows, I did.
They were all lining up to have a bit of this.
There was, um, Sharon at work.
That girl from the café down the street.
Um, your sister,
both of them.
Yeah, and um, God there was loads,
I was just drowning in offers.
And I did 'em all.
Yep, every single one.

MY WIFE PEGGY

Little did she know that you were out the back smoking joints with
   your bridesmaids for half the night.

Oh shit!
Fuck, oh I wish I had told you before you went and died.
You are going to shit yourself when I—
oh fuck, have you shit yourself?
I read somewhere that when you die you,
everything in you just comes … out.
Please don't have shit yourself, Peg,
I don't wanna check
and I don't want the girls seeing you covered in …
just don't, hey?
From now until I figure all this out,
just don't shit yourself.

So yeah,
I spoke to Jimmy yesterday and you were right.
Of course you were right.
He's been fooling around with Natalie or Naomi or whatever her
   name is.
He just came right out and said it.
Yes, I gave him a serve.
Liz is a good egg and doesn't deserve to be screwed over like that.
I told Jimmy to expect a call from you sometime in the week,
so you better get up and get onto that Peg.
Come on, up you get.
No?
Just going to lay there … dead?
Suit yourself then.

Feel like having a dance, Peg?
Oh come on,
get up,
let's have a dance.
You gotta get up though cause I really don't wanna touch you,
so you gotta get up on your own.

Which was it babe?
Which one?

I think I'll get pissed, hey.
I mean, why not?
It's still my birthday,
I should be celebrating.
Come on Peg, let's get sloshed.
Ha, good word hey, sloshed?
Wonder what it even means, hey,
if it means getting pissed?
That's what I'll do tomorrow then;
look up just what the fuck sloshed means.
I mean I'll have nothing else to do.
I'll call in sick for work,
take the girls to school and then,
spend the day researching the word sloshed.
Oh, well that's after I tell our family and friends that you went and
    fucking died, Peg.
That's going to be a really great conversation to have again and
    again.
'Oh hey, Aunty Linda, it's George here.
You know, I married Peggy.
Oh, speaking of Peggy, she's dead hey.
Sometime last night I imagine.
Beats me, found her dead this morning.
Poor form too if you ask me,
dying on my birthday and all.
Oh hey, all is not lost,
I found out what sloshed means,
so things are looking up.'

Christ that woman hates me.
I still remember at our wedding,
she just sat, sulking, wouldn't talk to no-one.
Found out later that she'd been going around telling everyone how
    you could do better than me.

MY WIFE PEGGY

She hated being pregnant.
Hated it.
Can't blame her though,
swollen ankles and neither of the girls sat well,
they both wanted to move about
and always at night.
I think there were a few months there,
with the first one,
where she only got like two hours sleep a night.
But then she got really sick.
We didn't know what was wrong for a while there
then the doctor ran some tests
and it turned out that she had gestational diabetes.
No family history of it, so we both got a bit of a shock
She took it in her stride though;
she wanted them kids, no matter what.

Remember the delivery, Peg?
Yeah I know you do.
Me getting a bit too excited and wanting to take photos of the main
    event
and you yelling at me that I wasn't allowed to take pictures of your
    vagina.

Sorry Peg, still makes me laugh.

Got a shock though
when the doctor asked if I wanted to take a look.
Down I went,
thinking I could handle anything
and then there it was,
BOOM,
stretched and bloody with Jessie's head starting to poke out.
Did I pass out then or with Nicole?
I can't remember hey,
you'd know though,
you gotta remember.

Be a pretty dull life without them though,
without my girls.
When they were young,
well, younger than they are now,
I used to have long hair.
Almost a mullet, if you can believe.
And the girls always wanted to put my hair in pigtails.
'Please Daddy. Please. Please. Please. Please. Please.'
On and on they would plead,
all the while knowing that I would give in.
I don't care what kind of man you think you are,
if your little girls want to put your hair in pigtails
and they give you the sweet little innocent eyes,
there ain't any way you're going to say no.

When our eldest, Jessica, was little she always wanted to play tea
    parties with me.
Peg would watch Jessie waiting by the window all afternoon,
tea set laid out, toys in place, just waiting for me.
She always just wanted to play tea parties with her dad. Jessie's
    always been mine.
We get each other.
Even from a young age she just seemed to want to be everywhere
    that I was.
Used to really piss Peg off until the second one came along.
It was almost as if I got the first one and Peg got the second.
Well that's how Peg made it feel like.
Jessie was mine and our second, Nicole, she's Peg's.
I wasn't interested in playing favourites though.
Honestly, I love them both.
I'm just happy they are healthy and happy girls.
And I know Peg loves them.
Loves them both.
Don't ya?
Deep down I know you love 'em both.
Couldn't ask for a better mum, could they, hey?

MY WIFE PEGGY

I wish my mum had said where he had gone, my pop.
Didn't need to be heaven but just somewhere.
Somewhere nice.
That's what I'm going to do for my girls,
'Your mum's gone somewhere nice and one day,
a long time from now,
you'll go there too and then,
we'll all be together again.
One day we'll be a family again.'

Fuck, I've been a bloody lucky man.
Ending up with the kids that I have.
I didn't know how I was going to be as a dad,
never done it before see.
But when our first one was born
and I held her and she was still covered in blood and bits of Peg,
well I thought,
'Hey, how hard can this be?'
And maybe we just got lucky,
but raising my girls has been a piece of cake.
Ha, piece of cake.

I mean, yeah, sometimes they shit me
and I imagine what my life would be like without them
and, sometimes that life,
a life without them,
it looks pretty good.
It would just be me and Peg.
Maybe we'd go overseas backpacking
or just buy a van and drive round the country.
And sometimes I used to think about what my life would be like
    without any of them.
I'd be a free man to do what I want, just live how I like.
I'm not the kind of guy who'd go wild,
but I just imagine the freedom,
the space to move,
to breathe.
Space to just be on my own.

'He's gone away.
Death is when you go away
and you don't come back.'
No heaven, no talk of an afterlife, nothing,
just told me that death takes people away.
The more I questioned the worse it got
till finally she just snapped
She burst into tears and ran out of the room.
I felt so guilty.
I could hear her crying from the bathroom.
She locked herself in and wailed, howling with grief.
The pain that was coming through that door was thick, heavy.
I thought I had caused it, her pain.
What else do you think when you're a kid?

I wasn't allowed to go to his funeral either.
Too young, everyone kept on saying,
but I wish they had all just let me decide that for myself.
It would have helped.
Helped to understand what it looks like.
Death.
I don't mean the body,
I'm glad I didn't see his body,
but I wish I could have seen that it's nothing to be scared of,
that it's a part of life.

When you're that young
and someone says that death is when you have to go away
and never come back,
suddenly it's something to be scared of.
And then the more that life goes on the scarier the idea of death is.
Took me years to just come to terms with the idea of my own death.
I'm not a particularly religious man
but I like to believe that there is something else.
You have to have it, don't you?
Something to believe in.
Otherwise nothing about it makes much sense.

MY WIFE PEGGY 5

I don't know whether I can move your body.
Whether I should even attempt to move your body.
I don't wanna touch you, Peg.
I don't want to feel your lifeless body falling into my arms.
But I can't leave you here.
Laying there the way you are.
If the girls find you like this.
Fuck.
What do you want me to say to the girls?
They ain't going to understand.
You bloody go and check out early and I have to teach them what
    death is.
'Morning girls so, this is what death looks like.
Take a good look at your mum there.
That's death.
Right there.
On the couch.'
Fucking hell Peg, you couldn't have done this in the bedroom?
I could have at least shut the door then.
Kept them out.
Bought some time till I got you looking decent.
Pulled the blanket up to your chin and brushed your hair
They'd remember you looking beautiful
and would never have to see their mum dead on the bloody couch.

I remember the first time I knew what death was.
My pop died when I was eight
and I remember my mum telling me that he had been very sick
and had died through the night.
'But where has he gone?'
I kept asking her over and over again.
'Where has Pop gone?'
Mum wasn't ready to tell me.
She meant well, she really did, but she just was too … raw.
To me he was just Pop,
but to her, that was her dad.
She kept telling me,

You weren't easy though, Peg.
Some people tell you that they have baggage,
but fuck, she came with a whole luggage cart.
Gambling mostly, bit of the drink as well.
It eased off after the girls came but still,
on the odd day, I'd come home from work
and she'd be gone, kids at her mum's place.
She's a bloody good mum,
but then there she'd be,
at the RSL, hitting the machines.
I wouldn't mind so much if she had a job of her own.
If it was her bloody fucking money that she was using but,
I'm the one punching out eight, sometimes ten-hour days and …
sorry, shouldn't speak so ill of the dead.
I gotta say Peg, I'm not happy about this, you going first.
It wasn't part of the plan.
See, I always wanted to go first.
I had this image of you finding me in my chair,
years from now,
and there I'd be, dead.
TV remote control in the one hand
and stubby in the other.
And you'd know exactly what to do.
You'd kiss my forehead,
and wouldn't find kissing a dead body gross.
You'd go to the kitchen and call the girls.
They'd want to rush over but you'd stop them,
telling them to come in the morning.
And then we'd just sit, together.
You in your chair and me,
dead as a doorknob in mine.
And it would be perfect.
A perfect moment.

Then you had to go and fuck it up, didn't you hey?
Tell me hey, what am I meant to do now?
I'm not prepared for this.

MY WIFE PEGGY

And it's sharp too.
Got a sharp taste to it.
Like glass.
I feel like I'm swallowing glass with every bite.
I'd imagine if you opened up my throat
you'd see it all torn up and raw,
with tiny bits of glass sticking out of the wounds.

We weren't high school sweethearts or anything.
We met at a party.
A mate of mine had a birthday party at his place;
God, would be twelve years ago now.
Fuck. Twelve years.
But yeah, he had a party at his place
and I turned up after work
and there she was.
I didn't leave her side all night.
I wasn't a dick or anything;
I just made sure she knew I was interested.
We both got a bit drunk,
Peggy has never been great on the booze,
but at the end of the night she wanted my number
and later the next week we had coffee.

When I looked at her with sober eyes
and listened to her talk
and laughed at her jokes
and she laughed at my terrible dad jokes,
I knew,
I knew that that was the woman I was going to marry.
On our next date she made me a cake
and after just one bite, that was it.
In no time we were dating
and then we got engaged.
It felt a bit rushed but you know,
you gotta put a ring on it if you like it, right?
Not sure I got that right, hey Peg?

And who's going to make my birthday cake now, hey? Didn't think
about that did ya, Peg?

It's my birthday.
Well, was.
Yesterday.
It was my birthday.
Forty-two.
I'm fucking forty-two years old.
And God, do I feel it?
She keeps me young though,
Peggy does, and the girls.
I got two little girls.
Little ratbags more like.
But I love them.
Fuck I don't think I could love those girls more.
They are the strongest, smartest and …

Boiled chocolate cake.
Don't get much better than that.
I'd never had one, not till I met Peggy.
Didn't even know that you could do that.
My nan used to boil a pudding,
which I guess is kind of a cake,
but nothing like this.
She never puts frosting on it either.
She likes to let the cake speak for itself.

She used to tell me that the secret ingredient was love
but I found out a few years ago that it was actually a shot of brandy.
Never told her that though, that I knew.
Would have broken my heart to see the look on her face.

I really shouldn't be eating so much of this.
I can't even taste it anymore.
It's too sweet.
It wasn't this sweet earlier in the night but now,
now it has that sweetness makes your teeth fuzzy.

Lights up on GEORGE, *sitting in an armchair, leaning over a coffee table eating cake. There is a bottle of red wine and a half-full glass on the side table.*

GEORGE: Look at her.
　　I often find her there, asleep.
　　We have a huge bed. Massive.
　　And I don't mind saying that I am an excellent big spoon.
　　No really, I dare you to find someone better at spooning than me.
　　It's all in the arm placement, you see.
　　You can't have your arm on an odd angle or it'll go numb,
　　but you gotta keep it just under the little spoon's head,
　　so they get the added neck support but it's not uncomfortable.
　　She's the best little spoon, my Peggy is.
　　Curls in real tight and close to you.
　　That's pretty much why we ended up with our second kid.
　　She curled in like she always does and I couldn't help myself.

　　But you can guarantee, without fail, that at some point in the night,
　　　　she'll end up right here, on the couch.
　　She tells me it's not me, that I shouldn't take it personally.
　　She's always done it, she says, even when she was a little girl.
　　It's a comfort thing she says.
　　She finds couches comforting.
　　That's my Peggy for ya, she says the craziest things,
　　but somehow, coming out of her mouth, they make sense.

　　She's dead, by the way. Peggy is. Dead.
　　I got up to take a piss and like always, she's on the couch.
　　I walk over to give her a kiss and she's cold.
　　I get up to take a piss and my wife's dead on the couch.

　　Could have picked a better night to do it, Peg.
　　Ruined my fucking birthday you have, Peg.

CHARACTER

GEORGE, mid 40s, Peggy's husband

SETTING

George and Peggy's lounge room, early hours of the morning.

My Wife Peggy was first staged at Gasworks Arts Park Studio Theatre, Melbourne, on 28 August, 2019, with the following cast:

GEORGE   Dallas Palmer

Writer and Director, Gavin Roach
Sound Designer, Connor Ross
Lighting Designer, Clare Springett

Contents

MY WIFE PEGGY   1

Theatre Program at the end of the playtext

CURRENT THEATRE SERIES

First published in 2022
by Currency Press Pty Ltd,
PO Box 2287, Strawberry Hills, NSW, 2012, Australia
enquiries@currency.com.au
www.currency.com.au

in association with Gavin Roach

Copyright: *My Wife Peggy* © Gavin Roach, 2022.

COPYING FOR EDUCATIONAL PURPOSES
The Australian *Copyright Act 1968* (Act) allows a maximum of one chapter
or 10% of this book, whichever is the greater, to be copied by any educational
institution for its educational purposes provided that that educational institution
(or the body that administers it) has given a remuneration notice to Copyright
Agency (CA) under the Act.

For details of the CA licence for educational institutions contact CA,
11/66 Goulburn Street, Sydney, NSW, 2000; tel: within Australia 1800
066 844 toll free; outside Australia 61 2 9394 7600; fax: 61 2 9394 7601;
email: info@copyright.com.au

COPYING FOR OTHER PURPOSES
Except as permitted under the Act, for example a fair dealing for the purposes
of study, research, criticism or review, no part of this book may be reproduced,
stored in a retrieval system, or transmitted in any form or by any means without
prior written permission. All enquiries should be made to the publisher at the
address above.

Any performance or public reading of *Gavin Roach* is forbidden unless a
licence has been received from the author or the author's agent. The purchase of
this book in no way gives the purchaser the right to perform the play in public,
whether by means of a staged production or a reading. All applications for public
performance should be addressed to the author c/- Currency Press

Typeset by Currency Press.
Printed by Fineline Print + Copy Services, Revesby, NSW.
Cover image by Helen Rofe.
Cover design by Mathias Johansson for Currency Press.

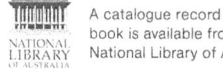 A catalogue record for this
book is available from the
National Library of Australia

MY WIFE PEGGY

Gavin Roach

CURRENCY PRESS
The performing arts publisher

GAVIN ROACH